Dear Vivas,

Wish you all the
Best!

[signature]

PRAISE FOR *THE MONEY TALK*

"*Money Talk* is a very timely and practical guide to retirement planning, specially written for the Indian American community. Rajesh Jyotishi is master storyteller. He makes such a dry subject as financial planning a joy to read."

—Jagdish N. Sheth, *Kellstadt Professor of Business, Emory University*

"Indians are so busy focusing on working hard to earn their wealth, but very few think about protection of their wealth. In my mind, this is very dangerous. Rajesh's book *Money Talk* addresses the importance of wealth preservation and gives our community multiple ways to protect their hard-earned wealth for future generations."

—Chandra (CK) I. Patel, *President, BVM Holdings; AAHOA Chairman 2010 Emeritus; and past board of director of US travel and tourism*

"As an estate planning attorney with over ten years of experience, I can't emphasize enough the importance of proper financial planning. Often, in my practice, I see that the South Asian women, and even those who hold high-paying jobs and have a great professional career before them, are clueless when it comes to financial planning. Many don't even know what assets they have, how much they own, and how they are held. To make matters worse for the Indian women, it is typically considered ill-fate and a bad omen to talk about their spouses' death and as such, many of the women do not like to discuss estate planning and family finances. As a result, with the unfortunate and unforeseen deaths of their spouses, they are left as beneficiaries or heirs of estates with no knowledge of family finances.

With the publication of this book, Rajesh hopes to reach out to as many people as possible including Indians and South Asians so that they are better informed and also well prepared for the challenges that they may face. I wish him the very best as he continues to expand his vision and commitment and work toward the betterment of our community as a whole."

—Shilpa Gokare, *attorney, Gokare Law Firm*

"This book could not have come at a better time, as the first big wave of Indian immigrants that came in the seventies and eighties are retiring and the next big wave of software professionals that came in the late nineties are already making aggressive plans for retirement. Rajesh's personal belief in the concept of giving that he always practiced is known to me. His advice to make charitable giving an integral part of the retirement planning is extremely valuable. A must-read for all immigrants!"

—Vijay Vemulapalli, *secretary and board of director, Vibha (www.vibha.org)*

"*Money Talk* by Rajesh Jyotishi is a timely, relevant, and easy-to-understand guide for financial planning for Indian Americans and others. It provides readers with the necessary information for the evaluation of their current financial status and suggests steps to ensure a worry-free financial future.

Indian society is changing, but life in many ways is still governed by tradition, conventions, and historical precedents. Gradually, laws are being enacted to protect property rights, encourage entrepreneurship, and eliminate corruption, but it still has a long way to go. In the US, on the other hand, there are laws, rules, and regulations covering almost every part of life—personal and commercial. Indian Americans are, relatively speaking, better educated than other immigrants and should not take things for granted out of inaction but take advantage of the existing laws and opportunities to plan for their own financial security and other family members. Serious reading of this book is the first step, as it opens one's eyes to the reality around us in our adopted country."

—Pavittar Safir, CFP

"I have found the Indian community to be by and large very intelligent and savvy when it comes to running their businesses and maintaining a close-knit family structure. Just as you may have a family doctor and dentist that you maintain a relationship with on your health, a competent, experienced, and ethical financial advisor can be worth their weight in gold in bringing it all together for you. With their expertise, whether it's about charitable giving, legacy planning, risk mitigation through diversification, or alternative investment strategies, these are not issues the common person has to deal with on a daily basis. I would highly encourage your readers to engage someone they can relate to and take that step to consult with one."

—Harsh (Harry) Mehra, ChFC, CRPC, AIF

"Rajesh's book, *Money Talk: Retirement and Estate Planning for Indian Americans*, is very informative and covers the two topics that everyone should consider. This book is a great resource and is invaluable to our Indian American community."

—Patty Krishnan, CPA, *owner, Krishnan Company PC CPA*

THE

MONEY
TALK

RAJESH JYOTISHI

THE
MONEY
TALK

RETIREMENT & ESTATE PLANNING FOR
INDIAN AMERICANS

Advantage®

Published by Advantage, Charleston, South Carolina.
Member of Advantage Media Group.

ADVANTAGE is a registered trademark, and the Advantage colophon is a trademark of Advantage Media Group, Inc.

Printed in the United States of America.

ISBN: 978-1-59932-543-9
LCCN: 2017931857

Cover design by Katie Biondo.

This publication is designed to provide accurate and authoritative information in regard to the subject matter covered. It is sold with the understanding that the publisher is not engaged in rendering legal, accounting, or other professional services. If legal advice or other expert assistance is required, the services of a competent professional person should be sought.

Advantage Media Group is proud to be a part of the Tree Neutral® program. Tree Neutral offsets the number of trees consumed in the production and printing of this book by taking proactive steps such as planting trees in direct proportion to the number of trees used to print books. To learn more about Tree Neutral, please visit **www.treeneutral.com.**

Advantage Media Group is a publisher of business, self-improvement, and professional development books. We help entrepreneurs, business leaders, and professionals share their Stories, Passion, and Knowledge to help others Learn & Grow. Do you have a manuscript or book idea that you would like us to consider for publishing? Please visit **advantagefamily.com** or call **1.866.775.1696.**

To my parents, Pramila and Chittaranjan Jyotishi,
for putting up with all of my madness;
to my wife, Pari, for supporting me in all of my ventures;
and to my boys, Shalin and Shreyas, who never cease to amaze me!

TABLE OF CONTENTS

xiii   Foreword

xv   Acknowledgments

1   Introduction

11   **Chapter 1:** Welcome to America–My Story!

21   **Chapter 2:** Money and Retirement

29   **Chapter 3:** The Seven Biggest Hurdles in Retirement

45   **Chapter 4:** Four Biggest Lessons Learned from the Crisis of 2008

51   **Chapter 5:** Six Insurance Questions Asked after My Motorcycle Accident

59   **Chapter 6:** Of Time and Money

67   **Chapter 7:** Saving for Retirement

77   **Chapter 8:** The Ultimate Retirement Plan

87   **Chapter 9:** Planning for Retirement Income

103   **Chapter 10:** Long-Term Care and the Desi Community

113   **Chapter 11:** Health Insurance Planning for Parents Moving to the United States from Abroad

119   **Chapter 12:** Basics of Estate Planning

135   **Chapter 13:** Planning for Estate Taxes

141   **Chapter 14:** Advanced Estate Planning

151   **Chapter 15:** Leaving a Charitable Legacy

159 **Chapter 16:** Six Lessons for My Kids and You

167 **Namaste:** How Can I Help?

171 **FREE Gift of Carpe Diem CD**

173 **Appendix A:** Survey Results: what are your Two Biggest Worries when it comes to Retirement?

177 **Appendix B:** Survey Results: Money Talk for Teens

FOREWORD

It matters not how strait the gate,

How charged with punishments the scroll.
I am the master of my fate:

I am the captain of my soul.

—WILLIAM ERNEST HENLEY

At the very outset, let me tell you that this book, *The Money Talk*, is not a superficial, candy-floss approach to financial planning. Before you finish the first couple of chapters, they will hit you pretty hard in the gut. You can be the world's greatest scientist, doctor, or engineer, with an excellent grip on your profession, but your life will be pretty worthless if you haven't defined your life's purpose and planned to reach that purpose!

The intent of this book is to wake you up out of your apathy. It is to assist you in shaping new choices, new directions, and new actions. And the Indian American community certainly needs to address this—to view money as a means toward an end rather than an end in itself. They need to define their goal and plan for it, and this book helps you do that with succinct concepts and case studies to open your mind.

To doubting Thomases who don't want to look in the mirror: put this book away right now! But for you—the open-minded reader, eager to learn—when you finish and apply the content of this book to your life, you will not only create an effective future but will also make your life more worthwhile.

Notwithstanding the plethora of books on financial planning—both serious and fluffy—this is one book that you will not want to put down until you finish it. It is the type of book that you will want to read, underline, and share with close relatives and friends.

To elucidate some specifics, Rajesh conceived the contents of *The Money Talk* with the Indian American in mind. He deftly addresses retirement planning, long-term care planning, health insurance planning, estate planning, and legacy/charitable-giving planning in this thorough and articulated guidebook that will help carve out your financial future.

I have known Rajesh as his coach and mentor for nearly fifteen years. He is sincere, goal-directed, and innovative in his approach. He researches and investigates concepts deeply before presenting them. He is multitalented and loves to discover new passions and to "reach higher than his grasp" in every area of his life. His greatest quality is his humility—to learn, to accept, to serve, and to understand.

This book is a testimony of Rajesh's qualities, skills, and educated experiences.

Make it a handbook for reshaping your future—you will be thankful you did!

—Mohan Kapur, executive / performance / career coach and speaker
Atlanta, GA, USA

ACKNOWLEDGMENTS

It is said that there is no such thing as original thought. Just as musicians are influenced by the musicians they are inspired by and have listened to, financial advisors are influenced by the people, books, and teachers they have had the opportunity to interact with.

The secret to my success has always been a great team. This has been true with our employee-benefits partners, our insurance partners, our investment-company partners, and the team we had while publishing *Khabar* magazine.

I have been blessed to have had many teachers over the years. I would like to thank all of them for the valuable insights they have shared with me. I am also grateful for the smart, savvy clients I serve who are willing to share their knowledge and experiences with me so that I can be better educated and able to serve others.

With these sentiments in mind, special thanks to my attorney friends Sonjui Kumar and Shilpa Gokare for helping me review the estate-planning section in this book.

I would also like to thank Mr. Mohan Kapur for his very generous foreword. Mr. Kapur has coached and mentored me and our team for many years, and I am grateful for his insights and wisdom through the years.

Finally, I would like to thank all of the editors and designers at Advantage for their persistence, patience, and attention to detail so we could put forth a book I can really be proud of.

INTRODUCTION

You can only become truly accomplished at something you love. Don't make money your goal. Instead, pursue the things you love doing, and then do them so well that people can't take their eyes off you.

—MAYA ANGELOU

Hello everybody. Namaste. My name is Rajesh Jyotishi. Welcome to *The Money Talk: Retirement and Estate Planning for Indian Americans*. Just to give you a little background about myself, I have been in the insurance and financial-services industry for over twenty-five years. I was co-owner and publisher of a magazine called *Khabar* (meaning "news" or "what's happening"), which has served the Indian American community in Georgia for about twenty-four years. I am no longer a co-owner of *Khabar*, as I sold my shares of the magazine in 2013 to my business partners, but I continue to host "Moneywise," the magazine's financial column.

As a lifelong student and learner, I guess you can say I have done a lot of interesting things. In addition to my financial-services business and the magazine, when I was much younger, I was a rock musician. I recorded my own CD of songs that I have written through the years, called *Carpe Diem,* which means "seize the day" in Latin. *Carpe Diem* is available on iTunes, Amazon, and many other online retailers, but I would like to offer it to you as a free gift that you are welcome to download for free from my music website at www. RJ-Music.com or www.RajeshJyotishi.com, where you can also read my story and read the lyrics to my songs. As someone once said, my songs will tell you more about me than I ever will.

I also love motivational and inspirational stuff. Over the last thirty years, I have probably gone through over a thousand nonfiction books on motivation, spirituality, business, and what makes us tick in the ways we do.

I wanted to write this book to commemorate my twenty-five years in the financial-services industry. And for my first book, I wanted to write specifically for the Indian American community in the United States. For the last quarter century, I have had the honor and privilege of serving the Indian American community in Georgia and surrounding areas, not only for their insurance, investment, financial-planning, and employee-benefits needs but also through our magazine *Khabar,* which is one of the largest print publications in Georgia and the surrounding areas for Indian Americans and South Asians with an estimated readership of about ninety thousand readers monthly. You can find out more about *Khabar* at www.Khabar.com.

Our community has done quite well for itself, wouldn't you agree? According to the 2015 US Census, Indian Americans are among the most affluent minority communities in the United States.[1] The median income for an Indian American household is

---

1   "List of ethnic groups in the United States by household income," Wikipedia, https://en.wikipedia.org/wiki/List_of_ethnic_groups_in_the_United_States_ by_household_income.

$101,591. When we compare that to the median income in the U.S. of $55,775, it is quite impressive.[2] Wouldn't you agree? The 2015 census also showed that there are an estimated 3.18 million Indian Americans in the United States, making our community the third-largest Asian American group, following Chinese Americans at 4.01 million and Filipino Americans at 3.42 million.[3]

If we look at all of the different sectors of our economy, we find Indian Americans thriving in many areas, including the hospitality industry, healthcare, small businesses, Internet and software services, as well as other professions.

Some of the CEOs of top US companies are Indian, such as Sundar Pichai of Google, Satya Nadella of Microsoft, and Indra Nooyi of PepsiCo, to name just a few. Our current surgeon general, Dr. Vivek Murthy, is Indian American. Interestingly, according to Spellingbee.com, all the National Spelling Bee champions from 2008 to 2016 have been Indian Americans.

We are also seeing more people of Indian descent in the entertainment and media fields. Actors like Kunal Nayyar of *The Big Bang Theory*, Priyanka Chopra of *Quantico*, and comedian Russell Peters are almost household names.

We are even seeing more politicians of Indian origin in government offices, such as Bobby Jindal, former governor of Louisiana; Nikki Haley, governor of South Carolina and Donald Trump's nominee for UN Ambassador; and Dr. Seema Verma, Donald Trump's nominee for administrator of Medicare and Medicaid services.

---

2   "US Household Income," Department of Numbers, http://www.deptofnumbers.com/income/us/.

3   "Demographics of Asian Americans," Wikipedia, https://en.wikipedia.org/wiki/Demographics_of_Asian_Americans.

In light of the sheer number and relative affluence of Indian Americans in the United States, we as a community have the ability to contribute significantly to this great country.

Indeed, we have a lot to be proud of. But at the same time, let's face it: We also have the same challenges as anyone else living in this country. We are seeing a rise in desi divorce rates. We are seeing more bankruptcies within the Indian community, and many of our retirees have found themselves insufficiently prepared for their retirement years and living off Social Security benefits and relying on Medicaid for healthcare support. I would also have to say that only a small percentage of our community has done any long-term care planning.

Some of the things we will be discussing in this book are challenges we all have to face at some time in our lives. For example, we will discuss the Indian American mind-set and what we value in chapter 1. In chapter 2, we will discuss our relationship with money and what we need to keep in mind while planning our retirement. In chapter 3, we will discuss the seven biggest hurdles in retirement, including longevity, inflation, taxes, Social Security, and Medicare. In chapter 4, we will discuss the four biggest lessons learned from the crash of 2008.

As a side note, some interesting things happened to me while I was writing this book. For one, I was involved in a motorcycle accident. In fact, a part of this book was typed with one hand, because my right hand was in a splint for some time. In chapter 5, I'll share with you the six biggest insurance lessons that came to me while I was in the emergency room in a CAT scanner.

As we go along, I will share not only some of our challenges but also some solutions—I will introduce the tools of retirement and estate planning and how you can use them to your benefit.

From chapters 6 to 12, we will also discuss the needs of the wealthy in our community. The wealthy have done a great job creating and accumulating wealth, but many haven't planned their estates properly, with the use of wills and trusts. Many of the wealthy in our community may find that a significant portion of their wealth will go to pay estate taxes unless they take some action to help minimize the effect.

In the estate-planning section (chapters 13 and 14), we will discuss the basic estate planning that we all should have in place, as well as the importance of wills, powers of attorney, and living wills. In chapter 14, Advanced Estate Planning, we will discuss some of the problems and solutions faced by multimillionaires, including how to reduce or eliminate estate taxes, some of the challenges of estate planning for non-US citizens, the threats to your children and grand-children, and some ideas to help you accomplish your charitable and philanthropic goals.

While I was writing this book, I also had an idea of doing an audio program called *The Money Talk for Teens,* to be recorded at the same time as the audio version of this book. So I created a survey of twelve questions and reached out to thousands of clients and friends from around the world in various professions, age groups, and wealth levels. I asked them for their input on the best advice they'd gotten on money and what advice they'd give to their teenagers.

The twelve basic questions I asked in the survey are as follows:

1. What is the best advice you have gotten regarding money and life?

2. What would you tell your teenager regarding the high cost of a college education?

3.   What advice would you give to your teenager who wants to enter the arts (such as acting or music) or sports?

4.   What advice would you give on marriage and money?

5.   What advice would you give on spending and frugality?

6.   What advice would you give on debt?

7.   What advice would you give on saving and investing?

8.   What advice would you give on welfare and entitlement programs?

9.   What information would you disclose regarding an inheritance from you?

10.   What advice would you give on giving and generosity?

11.   What do you expect from your children in your old age?

12.   In your own words, list three things that you would like me to convey to your teenager in this book.

The responses I got were fascinating and included many perspectives I hadn't even considered. I have incorporated some of that data in the back of this book as well, and I think you will find it very interesting.

The Money Talk for Teens is available on Amazon, iTunes, and other online retailers, but as another token of my appreciation, I would like to offer you a free download of the program on our website at www.RajeshJyotishi.com where you can also subscribe to my e-mail newsletter for important, timely articles on finances. You will also receive invitations for free educational webinars that we conduct on a periodic basis (on a variety of subjects such as health-care, insurance, financial planning, and specific insurance and investment products) in which I interview investment-company professionals about interesting new products that may be of help in your financial planning.

After my first survey got such a great response, I decided to do a second survey to find out your thoughts on retirement planning, estate planning, and long-term care. The data received from that survey was also fascinating, and I have included some of the survey questions and answers throughout this book as we talk about those subjects. The ten questions asked in the survey on retirement and estate planning are as follows:

1. What are your two biggest worries when it comes to retirement?

2. Do you plan on working in your retirement years?

3. Do you plan on retiring in the United States?

4. Do you feel you have saved enough for retirement?

5. What is the most important thing you look for in an investment product?

6. Do you have a long-term care plan in place for healthcare costs in retirement?

7. Have you done your estate planning?

8. Do you plan on living with your children in retirement?

9. Do you know how much money you will need for retirement?

10. In what areas do you need the most education?

    ☐ retirement planning

    ☐ estate planning

    ☐ insurance planning

- [ ] tax planning
- [ ] long-term care planning
- [ ] charitable giving

I would also suggest that if you are a man who makes the primary financial decisions in your house that you also share this book with your spouse because in our community (as well as many other communities), women are often left in the dark when it comes to family finances. In the event of a husband's death or disability, the surviving spouse is left with limited knowledge of where everything is, and in many cases that proves to be an additional traumatic experience on top of the loss of a loved one.

The Money Talk represents the most important financial lessons I have learned over the last twenty-five years as an insurance agent and financial planner serving the Indian community. I guess you can say this book is part memoir, part practical knowledge that I have learned and would like to share, and part personal money philosophy and outlook on things that matter most. I have tried to make it an easy read for you, with interesting stories from my past, quotes from famous personalities on money, and case studies and examples that you may be able to relate to. There are often multiple ways to get from point A to point B, and who is to say what is right and wrong? We all have our own money philosophy that we live by, and I totally respect you for that!

My intention is to expand your knowledge and give you some food for thought while you plan out your future. I hope you find this book interesting, inspiring, and thought-provoking as you make your way through this thing called life.

If I can help in any way, please feel free to contact me. I would love to hear from you and what you thought about this book. You are also welcome to connect with me on Facebook, LinkedIn, Twitter, and our website at www.RajeshJyotishi.com.

CHAPTER 1

WELCOME TO AMERICA— MY STORY!

Gratitude is not only the greatest of virtues,
it is the parent of all others.

—CICERO

America is such a great country! She has given so many of us amazing opportunities for wealth, prosperity, and the pursuit of happiness. I think you will agree that there are very few countries in the world where one can come without much education or experience and still build an abundant life for his or her family.

The typical immigrant from India who came here in the 1960s, 1970s, and 1980s took a big step when deciding to venture off into a new country where nearly everyone was a stranger. Many had no idea how they were going to make a living and in many cases could barely speak English. The desi mind-set tends to focus on family, education, and safety, which I think is great. We should be focused on the well-being of our families and do what we can to provide for them in a protective way. That is what being prudent means. The Indian culture values family above all. This includes our children, our parents, our grandparents, and our extended family of uncles, aunts, cousins, and friends.

My father came to the United States as a student back in the late 1960s with just $8 in his pocket. As one of five brothers and two sisters, he ventured to this new land for the opportunity of a better life not only for himself but also for his brothers, sisters, and extended family. He worked multiple jobs after arriving here and at the same time studied to get two master's degrees in engineering.

After he was secure enough here, my father brought the rest of us over from India. My mother, my sister, and I came to the United States around 1971. I was only eight years old when we first came to the United States and literally knew just a handful of English words, such as "yes," "no," "thank you," and "please." I remember my mother asking me to watch television so that I could learn more English words. I am sure she must have regretted that afterward, as you couldn't tear me away from the TV while growing up.

We started our lives in New York City, like most Indian immigrants at that time. The process of immigration and green cards was easy back then, as the United States wanted new workers. There were not many English as a Second Language classes back then, so you pretty much had to learn on your own. We moved to Atlanta, Georgia, in 1974, when my father had a job opportunity working for an engineering firm: Parsons Brinckerhoff, Tudor, and Bechtel. Later he moved on to work with various defense-oriented companies such as Martin Marietta, Lockheed, Rockwell, Boeing, and EMS Technologies.

While my father was working his multiple jobs and traveling for work, he started an Indian grocery store for my mother to operate. It was named "Mira Enterprises," after our guru back in India. And let me tell you! An Indian grocery store in Atlanta back in the 1970s and 1980s was more of a community service than a thriving business opportunity. There was not a large Indian population in Atlanta at the time. I believe we had around 250 to 300 families back then. But to find authentic Indian groceries and fresh Indian vegetables— things we totally take for granted nowadays—was a treat, and it was appreciated by our community.

I remember working in my mother's grocery store on the weekends, packing spices and grains into plastic bags so we could sell them. Yes, we had to pack them ourselves, because we got them in bulk and had to make the small packages for customers. If you happened to have some really spicy red pepper, you had to be careful not to let it go up in the air, or you'd sneeze your head off!

We closed down the grocery store in the mid-1980s, but we made some great friends in the process while serving our community.

I remember being the only Indian kid in school while growing up and the awkwardness that came with that. I was a shy and introverted kid trying hard to fit in within a mostly white American community.

My first job outside of our family business was in our friend's Baskin-Robbins, where I worked part time for $3.45 an hour while going to college. My second job was with a company called Construction Market Data (CMD), where I started out at $4.00 an hour as the copy boy.

CMD published daily and weekly construction reports, and I was in charge of their production. Shortly after I started with them, they brought in printing presses and promoted me to production manager of the company, responsible for printing and mailing out their daily and weekly reports. After five or six years, I transferred to sales. I was with the company for about seven and a half years, and it was an awesome company to work for! I got to meet some amazing people I am still in touch with after thirty-plus years, and I learned some very important skills that are still applicable in my life today.

After I left CMD in 1990, I wanted to do something where I could be my own boss (like many of you). I wanted to have control of my own time, grow at my own pace, and have a sense of independence. Money was important, but not as important as all the rest. I accidentally stumbled upon the financial-services industry. I started out with New York Life as an insurance agent and after a couple of years decided to branch out on my own as a broker so that I could represent many companies and provide a wider spectrum of products and services.

Back in the early 1990s, there weren't many ways one could advertise and market to the Indian community in Georgia, so a couple of friends (Parthiv and Mehul Parekh) and I thought we would start something that would allow us to advertise to our community while also providing a way for other businesses in our community to advertise. That is how we launched *Khabar*. *Khabar* started as a coupon mailer, similar to Valpak, because there wasn't much news in our community at that time, as the community was still fairly small.

Because I was on great terms with my previous employer and knew how to print and mail, my friends at CMD would give me the key to their premises once a month, and we would take our own paper in, use their equipment, and be out by morning like a bunch of elves. We literally couldn't have started *Khabar* without their support, and for that I will eternally be grateful.

After the 1996 Olympics in Atlanta, the Indian community in Atlanta grew, especially with the looming Y2K crisis. Many Indian software programmers immigrated to Atlanta, as well as to other parts of the United States. Atlanta offered good weather, reasonable cost of living compared to other large cities, and an international airport, which made international travel much easier. The Indian community was also growing in other industries such as retail and hotels, as well as expanding opportunities for professionals such as doctors and engineers. With *Khabar*, we were in the right place and at the right time to grow with our community. *Khabar* evolved from a coupon mailer that reached just three thousand households, to a newsletter format with just sixteen pages, to a newsprint magazine in 1995, and eventually to a full-color, glossy magazine around 2004. It currently reaches around twenty-seven thousand households in Georgia and surrounding areas. I am proud to say it is still one of the most popular print magazines in Atlanta and surrounding areas. *Khabar* is a free print magazine for people in the state of Georgia, and everyone can subscribe to the free digital edition at www.Khabar. com.

During all those years, I was also learning and growing in the financial-services industry. I went through numerous certification programs including the Certified Estate Planner, Master Certified Estate Planner, Certified Senior Advisor, and Certified Long-Term Care, as well as the Financial Planner Program at Oglethorpe University in Atlanta, which is a prerequisite to become a Certified Financial Planner™. I love to learn, and these certifications were just part of learning and growing. For personal reasons, I currently do not hold any of the designations mentioned here, but I continue to invest a lot of time and money in my education.

In his book *Outliers*, Malcolm Gladwell talks about the "10,000-Hour Rule"—that it generally takes about ten thousand hours, or five years, of effort in your craft before you can get good at it. I would say this was very true for both my financial-services business and our publication. We made a lot of mistakes along the way, but we also learned from them and made constant and never-ending improvements.

I share all of this with you with total humility, just to let you know that I too understand what it is like to struggle, work hard, make some mistakes, and learn from them ("fail forward") to come up in life slowly, over time. I also understand the mind-set of some of your children, affectionately called ABCDs (American-Born Confused Desis), who are probably more like me when it comes to our Indian culture: even though I was born in India, I have been raised here in the United States for the majority of my life.

THE INDIAN MIND-SET

An investment in knowledge pays the best interest.

—BENJAMIN FRANKLIN

If you asked most members of our community what they value the most, you would probably hear the word "family" more often than not. Our community values family above many other things. This is not to say that other cultures do not value their families, but historically, our culture and background consists of joint families, where parents live with their children once the children are grown and married, and the children take care of their parents during their golden years. Sometimes the entire family of brothers, along with their wives and children, live in a joint family household under the same roof as the parents. We don't see much of that in American families.

The tradition in most Western cultures is that when children are old enough, typically eighteen or older, they are required or encouraged to move out of their parents' home and start making their own lives. Indian parents, on the other hand, prefer to stay involved in their children's lives, pay for their children's college and wedding costs, help them with the down payments for their homes and cars, and be a support system for their children throughout their lives. We consider it our obligation and want to make sure our children aren't overly burdened with financial struggles while they are starting their careers, so we do what we can.

SURVEY: DO YOU PLAN ON RETIRING IN THE U. S. A.?

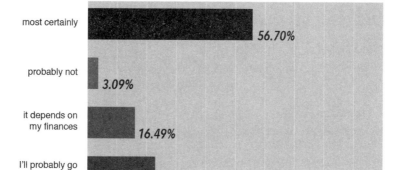

When it comes to retirement planning, our perspectives are also a little different than those in Western cultures. Maybe because we have seen our parents take care of our grandparents back home, there is some expectation that our children will also be there for us and take care of us in our retirement years.

As much as I would love it if my boys take care of me and my wife when we are older, I have to realize that things could be different when that time comes. Like it or not, things are a little different for us in the United States.

> *As much as I would love it if my boys take care of me and my wife when we are older, I have to realize that things could be different when that time comes. Like it or not, things are a little different for us in the United States.*

The times have changed. We are seeing a lot more divorces, even within Indian families. We are seeing both spouses having to work to make a living, and our children are sometimes required to travel and move to other parts of the world for work. They can't always be available for their parents in their time of need. That is why we must put plans in place so that, in the eventuality that our children are not able to take care of us in our golden years, we can take care of ourselves, financially and otherwise.

Many Indian Americans also believe that, in the event they need healthcare in their golden years or if they have not saved enough for retirement, they can always move back to India, where they can leverage their dollars to rupees, live quite comfortably with less money, and hire healthcare services at a fraction of what it would cost in the United States. But that is also changing.

If you talk to people in India, things are not all that cheap there anymore. It is difficult to find and maintain regular household help, and the cost of living is also rising, depending on what you are purchasing.

I still think that retiring in India is a viable option if you truly enjoy being in India, but keep in mind that living in India is not that easy for people who have been in the States for many years. There are many challenges and everyday hazards, including pollution, over-population, and corruption, as well as general hardships of day-to-day living. The amount of time and energy it takes to complete a simple task such as banking can take most of your day there.

Also ask yourself if you really want to be away from your children and grandchildren if they are living in the United States or other parts of the world. That is the type of question this book asks and addresses in every chapter. My job is to ask you the questions and let you form your own answers. That is a beauty of a question. When someone asks you a question, your mind automatically goes to find the solutions. That is what I have learned from my coaches and mentors. Ask questions, let your clients tell you what is most important to them, and then show them the solutions they are looking for.

I love the way Americans have given to other countries around the world in their time of need. Whenever there is a catastrophe of any sort, Americans are there, willing to give and donate without any expectations in return, and I am proud to be one of those individuals.

I am truly grateful for all of the opportunities this country has given me and my family. Sometimes, when we see or hear the word "opportunity," our mind goes automatically to careers, and by extension to finances. But that's not exactly the kind of opportunity I'm grateful for, although that is certainly part of it. What I really mean is the larger sense of the word—it's the opportunity for us as individuals, as families, and as a community to learn and grow, in every direction. This country has been very good to us, and we, in turn, contribute our mind-sets and our dreams.

CHAPTER 2

MONEY AND RETIREMENT

Money is a terrible master but an excellent servant.

—P.T. BARNUM

WHAT DOES MONEY MEAN TO YOU?

Here's an interesting question for you: What does money mean to you? Seriously, think about this for a minute. It's an important question because all of your actions and behaviors are tied to this central belief system, and it can mean different things to different people.

I know that for some people, money means safety and security. They believe that if they have enough of it, they don't have to worry about having to do without the essentials of life, such as food, shelter, and healthcare, and their family will be well taken care of and not have to suffer any discomforts. It's like a warm cozy blanket that you want to wrap around yourself for comfort.

For some people, money represents power. You know what I mean. When you have enough money, people take you seriously and give you respect. When you go anywhere, they are willing to wait on you and are always at your beck and call.

For some people, money means freedom. I can really relate to this, because that's what money means to me. It gives me the freedom to do whatever I want, whenever I want. If I want to go to a fancy restaurant every night and enjoy great food and wine, I'll do that. If I want to take a month off from work and travel to exotic, beautiful destinations around the world, I'll do that. If I want to buy a nice car just because, I'll do that!

You might even be saying to yourself, *You know what? I kind of like all of those things! I like the feeling of security that money brings me, I like the power associated with having abundance, and I like the freedom that is associated with having wealth.* And there is nothing wrong with that. So here is the next question for you.

CAN YOU EVER HAVE ENOUGH MONEY?

Money never made a man happy yet, nor will it. The more a man has, the more he wants. Instead of filling a vacuum, it makes one.

—BENJAMIN FRANKLIN

One thing I have noticed in watching myself and most people around the world is that we are always working toward getting *more*— more money, more knowledge, more influence, more status, more Facebook friends, more likes on our Facebook posts, more Twitter followers, and just generally more of everything.

If you are a millionaire, you want to become a multimillionaire. If you are a billionaire, you want to become a multibillionaire. If you are on a spiritual path and have had a small glimpse of what enlightenment might feel like, you want even deeper and longer-lasting spiritual experiences. And I don't think there is anything wrong with that—that's just the way most of us are wired. Whatever your choice of attraction is, whether it be power, money, or fame—the more of that you want.

For some people, money is like an addiction. Their whole life is consumed with having more of it. It's like an alcoholic who craves alcohol, an addict who can't get enough drugs . . . I think you get the message. And sadly, if you have any of the addictions mentioned here, money supports them all, too, making you want still more money.

SURVEY: DO YOU FEEL YOU HAVE SAVED ENOUGH FOR RETIREMENT?

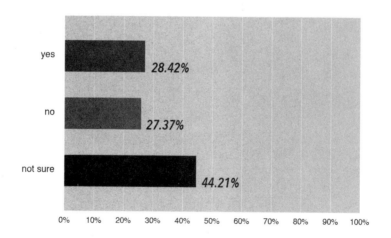

One lesson I have learned in life and in the financial-services industry is that when it comes to money, if you are not careful, it will *never* be enough. The never-ending pursuit of *more* will consume your life and rob you of the joy and happiness of having money in the first place. We have already seen how greed in the corporate world has crippled our economies at times.

But it doesn't have to be that way. What if you were clear about how much is enough for you? What if you knew the magic number you needed to retire comfortably and were on track to both reach and maintain that amount of money? Would that help alleviate some of your anxiety over money?

What if, when someone asked what your retirement goal is, you could answer with certainty and without hesitation? "My retirement goal is to be debt-free and have at least $2 million in investable assets that can provide a minimum of $100,000 a year for the rest of my life." I just made up those numbers as an example, but what if you had that type of clarity about your needs? Once you know your magic number, the rest is just math.

What if we could structure our lives based on what we need and set a strategy in place so that we can take more time to make sure our wheel of life is full in all areas? What if instead of focusing on having more money, we focused on having more time—the time needed to do the things that are most satisfying to us? Here is another interesting question for you.

WHAT DOES RETIREMENT MEAN TO YOU?

Don't simply retire from something; have something to retire to.

—HARRY EMERSON FOSDICK

Retirement means different things to different people. For some people, it means finally being able to do all the things they have wanted to do, like travel, spend more time with their grandchildren, pursue their hobbies, or launch a second career. For some, it may mean spending more time in spiritual activities or volunteering for charitable causes; for others, it may mean just doing a bunch of nothing! There is no wrong answer. It's your retirement. You should get to spend it the way you want.

A BRIEF HISTORY OF RETIREMENT IN AMERICA

While you are pondering this question, let me give you a brief history of retirement planning in America because it will give you a new perspective on retirement.

Retirement planning is actually a relatively new concept. We really didn't have the kind of retirement we are accustomed to now until after World War II in this country. Prior to that, in the years leading up to the Great Depression, people pretty much worked their entire life or until they couldn't do their task anymore.

During the Great Depression, corporations needed to get older workers out in order to create jobs for younger individuals entering the workforce, and many offered their workers an early retirement package. Many of the workers who took the package didn't realize it was optional.

What followed was that many people who had retired lost their sense of purpose. Their whole life and identity was tied to their work. In many cases, even their social life was tied to their colleagues at work. Once they lost that purpose, and without something else filling its place, many of them just died after a few years, out of depression and lack of purpose.

Of course, we now live in a world where retirement is something many people eagerly look forward to. Many of you also may still want to work in some capacity in your retirement years, and that is also perfectly fine. Personally, I would always like to be working in some capacity. Maybe not a full-time activity, but I would like to stay active.

SURVEY: DO YOU PLAN ON WORKING IN YOUR RETIREMENT YEARS?

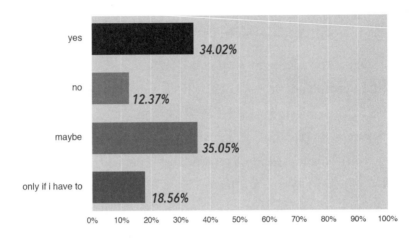

I love the fact that we now have more options than ever when it comes to retirement. You have the freedom to retire anywhere in the world. If you want to retire and spend half your time in India and half in the States, you can most certainly do that. If you want to go back and get a new college degree, you can do that.

You have the freedom to retire anywhere in the world. If you want to retire and spend half your time in India and half in the States, you can most certainly do that.

If you want to retire "around the world," you can even do that! In the world of Airbnb, HomeAway, and other home rental websites, it is literally possible to retire around the world. My wife and I would love to try that for a while. Imagine spending two to three months on a beautiful beach in the Caribbean, then moving to some snow-clad mountains in the Swiss Alps, then spending some time in Paris, France, and then moving on to Italy and other parts of the world. Yes, we would also go to India from time to time, but the world is a beautiful place, and we could take the time to explore it. The only limit is our imagination and of course money!

OWNERSHIP IS OVERRATED

Empty pockets never held anyone back. Only empty heads and empty hearts can do that.

—NORMAN VINCENT PEALE

I read an interesting Facebook post the other day. It started out with some questions and answers. The first question was "What is the biggest hotel chain in the world that owns no hotels?" The answer was Airbnb. The second question was "What is the biggest taxi company in the world that owns no taxis?" The answer was Uber. And the third question was "What is the biggest media company in the world that doesn't create any content?" The answer was Facebook. It's pretty profound how our world has changed in the last few decades, isn't it?

One lesson I learned a long time ago was that ownership is oftentimes overrated, especially if you are not going to be using that item on an ongoing, consistent basis. Let me give you a quick example.

Many years ago, I wanted to buy a boat. My kids were young and we live in Atlanta, where we are pretty close to

Lake Lanier, and I thought that this would be a fun thing for our family to have and enjoy as they grew up. While I was doing my research on what type of boat to buy, I talked to a few people who owned boats, and some of them told me that the two happiest days in a boat owner's life are when he buys the boat and he sells the boat—because there is a lot of work involved in owning a boat. You have to store it, you have to clean it, and you have to maintain it, and if you're only using the boat once in a while, then whenever you're not on it, you're working on upkeep. So what's a guy to do who wants to have a boat?

Well, interestingly, I found out there are boat clubs where you pay an initiation fee and a monthly membership fee, sort of like a golf membership, and whenever you go out on a boat, you pay for your gas. On top of that, the boat club has a wide variety of boats, including pontoons, bow riders, deck boats, and cabin cruisers that they not only maintain but also replace with new ones periodically to keep the inventory up-to-date and members happy. I thought this was an awesome idea, so about ten years ago, I joined a boat club here called Freedom Boat Club. The club also has franchises in several states, so if we want to get a boat while we are in Florida, Michigan, New York, or other places where they have a branch, we just have to call them up and, if there is availability, just go enjoy! We get all of the joy and none of the hassle of ownership.

Now, I am not trying to sell you a boat club membership, but rather, I am trying to make a point. With today's technology and resources like HomeAway, you do not need to own everything in order to get the enjoyment of having it.

CHAPTER 3

THE SEVEN BIGGEST HURDLES IN RETIREMENT

It's not how much money you make but how much money you keep,
how hard it works for you, and how many generations you keep it for.

—ROBERT KIYOSAKI

Let me ask you a very interesting question. If you had to climb Mount Everest, the tallest mountain in the world, would you consider yourself a success once you reached the top? If you said yes, you would only be half right.

In order for you to be truly successful, you would need to reach the top of the mountain and also come down safely. Wouldn't you agree? Most people do not know that Everest actually claims more lives on the descent than it does on the climb.

Retirement planning is sort of like climbing Everest. It is not enough that we make it to retirement; we also need to make sure we get through retirement safely.

Here are the seven biggest hurdles in retirement that you will need to be aware of and prepared for during your retirement years.

HURDLE 1–OUTLIVING YOUR INCOME

Money is only a tool. It will take you wherever you wish, but it will not replace you as the driver.

—AYN RAND

Many years ago, when I took the Certified Senior Advisor class mentioned in chapter 1, the instructor pointed out a very interesting fact. He asked, "Do you know what the fastest-growing segment of our population is right now?" We thought he was referring to ethnic groups, but the answer he was looking for was centenarians—yes, people over the age of one hundred!

With advances in healthcare and nutrition, people are living longer and longer. What used to kill us doesn't even slow us down much anymore. We all know of people who have had chronic ailments such as diabetes and high blood pressure and still lived into their nineties. I believe this trend is going to continue.

This means that if you were to retire at age sixty-five, you could potentially have thirty-plus years in retirement, which is kind of scary and exciting at the same time, isn't it? On one hand, the prospects of living a very long life could be exciting, as it could mean you will have more time to enjoy and do the things you want to do. But if your health is failing and your finances are deteriorating, you may have some challenges in store.

Unfortunately, we can't help you much when it comes to your health. That is something only you can take care of, with exercise and proper nutrition. Unfortunately, sometimes we are also subject to health conditions that are out of our hands such as cancer, genetics, and infectious diseases. But when it comes to your finances, we have many insurance and financial products that are designed specifically for seniors concerned about outliving their incomes, that can provide pension-like income for life, and that may also provide protection against potential healthcare costs in retirement.

For the Indian retiree who plans on retiring in other parts of the world besides the United States, you may want to look at products that can provide benefits around the world so that you can obtain long-term care when you need it, regardless of whether you are in the United States, India, or elsewhere. We will also discuss the need for long-term care in a little more detail later on.

HURDLE 2–THE CHALLENGE OF SOCIAL SECURITY

*At age twenty we worry what others think about us,
at forty we don't care what they think, and at sixty we
discover they haven't been thinking of us at all.*

—ANN LANDERS

You may be wondering why Social Security could be a challenge in retirement. Isn't Social Security an asset to a retiree as a supplemental income benefit—something we should be looking forward to? The answer is both yes and no. Yes, Social Security is a benefit that can provide some additional income, but there are also some major challenges for the Social Security Administration.

Social Security was enacted in 1935 by President Franklin D. Roosevelt to provide a supplemental income benefit to people over age sixty-five. At that time, the average life expectancy was just fifty-eight for men and sixty-two for women, and their benefits wouldn't begin until age sixty-five, so there were very few people receiving benefits in comparison to the number of people working.[4]

Today, life expectancies in the United States are around 76.9 years for men and 81.6 years for women.[5] In addition, the largest segment of our population, baby boomers (individuals born from 1946 to 1964), are now retiring by the millions each year and will be drawing benefits for an extended period of time.

People are living much longer, and the number of people contributing into the Social Security system may decrease as retirees stop working, which may cause a shortage in the future. This is a big concern for many.

We have already started to see changes in the minimum age requirement for full benefits. It used to be age sixty-five; it's now sixty-seven (depending on your birth year). For some time now, we have also seen Social Security as a taxable benefit for people in higher income tax brackets, whereas initially they were tax-free. Could the future bring age requirements of seventy, seventy-two, or higher? Could we see Social Security benefits reduced for people in the highest income brackets? Your guess is as good as mine, but it wouldn't surprise me if we were to see some changes.

---

4   Social Security Administration, "Social Security History," https://www.ssa.gov/history/lifeexpect.html.

5   "List of countries by life expectancy," Wikipedia, https://en.wikipedia.org/wiki/List_of_countries_by_life_expectancy.

HURDLE 3–HEALTHCARE EXPENSES

One of the biggest worries for a retiree are healthcare expenses. Especially in America! I remember several years ago, I was at one of our broker/dealer annual compliance meetings, and Alan Greenspan—then the chairman of the Federal Reserve—was one of the speakers. It was a very interesting talk.

The topic went to Social Security and Medicare. I'll never forget what Greenspan said about them. He said that Social Security is an easier problem for us to solve because we know how many people we have in this country. We know when they will be eligible for Social Security benefits, and based on actuarial science, we can calculate how many years we will need to pay for them.

But Medicare is a totally different issue. Medicare deals with health insurance. Healthcare costs can vary from state to state, and there is no way to predict the amount of healthcare expenses individuals may need. Some people may need $1 million in care, and others may not need any at all. We also don't know how long people will need the care or the future costs of that care, as medical inflation is accelerating at a much higher rate than consumer price-based inflation.

For those of you who are new to Medicare, it consists of several parts, which are as follows:

Medicare Part A: Part A provides coverage for hospitalization. Most people in the US are eligible for Part A when they turn sixty-five. But for immigrants, there is a requirement that you must have worked in this country and paid taxes for at least ten years, or forty quarters. If you have been a consistent permanent resident for at least five years, you may purchase Part A from the government, and the current costs in 2017 are $413 per month per person. This amount is indexed for inflation and goes up gradually every year. If you have worked for thirty or more quarters, you may be able to purchase at a lesser price. For more information, go to www.Medicare.gov.

Medicare Part B: Part B covers doctor visits, labs, X-rays, emergency ambulance services, routine physicals, and many other things. The Part B coverage only provides coverage for about 80 percent of the expenses. The remaining 20 percent becomes potentially an unlimited liability unless you fill the gap by purchasing additional Medicare supplement insurance or a Medicare Advantage Plan, which is referred to as Part C. The standard cost for Part B in 2017 is $137 per month per person and can be as high as $428.60 per month per person depending upon your income. Once again, to get exact numbers, go to www.medicare.gov.

Medicare Part C: Part C is provided by private insurance companies to fill some of the gaps in coverage that are in Medicare Parts A and B. Some of the gaps in Medicare include hospital deductibles, limitations on the number of days Medicare will pay for hospital stays, etc. There are many options for Medicare supplement plans and Medicare Advantage Plans, and the rates can vary significantly between them. It is best to seek out a good Medicare insurance agent to explain your options and help you choose a plan that suits your needs.

Medicare Part D: Then we have Medicare Part D, which covers prescription drugs and is also sold by private insurance companies, and rates can vary based on plan benefits. If you take multiple medications, Medicare.gov is a great place to compare plans and get recommendations for a good plans. But I would still recommend you find a good Medicare agent to help you choose a policy. Sometimes, there are certain nuances in differences. Some insurance companies may also offer additional wellness benefits such as gym memberships that you may not know while comparing rates online.

Confused yet? I don't blame you! I know all of this is very confusing. The challenge that we face with Medicare is that all of this comes with a cost, and the costs are going up. As we see more and more people retiring and living into their eighties, nineties, and hundreds, it would not surprise me if the costs associated with having Medicare supplement plans also rise to meet those expenses.

This doesn't even include the other part of healthcare expenses which is a real concern for many—the cost of long-term care expenses. I will discuss this concern in more detail in chapter 10, Long-Term Care, and the desi community. Also in chapter 11, I will go over health insurance options for people over age sixty-five who are not eligible for Medicare.

HURDLE 4—INFLATION

A nickel ain't worth a dime anymore.

—YOGI BERRA

Inflation is when the price of goods rises and the relative value of your money decreases. Do you remember when gasoline was under a dollar or a new home cost less than $50,000?

While growing up in the 1970s and 1980s, I occasionally watched the TV game show *The Price Is Right,* hosted at the time by Bob Barker. In the show, contestants are required to guess the price of various items, and the contestant who comes the closest to the correct price (without going over) wins some very nice prizes, such as cars, boats, and vacations.

While watching this show, I remember what the price of an average car was in the 1970s—brand-new, midpriced autos were in the $4,000 to $5,000 price range. Do you remember those days? Then the prices went up to $8,000–$10,000, then $15,000, and then $20,000, and they continue to get more and more expensive. This is an example of inflation.

For Indian Americans who have lived in India, I am sure you must have some fascinating stories of how much stuff you could buy for just one hundred rupees. Nowadays, one hundred rupees doesn't carry much weight. It's one of the smaller bills you carry while in India.

Now imagine the costs of goods and services twenty to thirty years in the future. What will be the cost of food, gas, and cars? And imagine what the cost of healthcare will be, as the inflation rate for that is higher than for consumer goods. It can be a little frightening to think about the future costs of our daily goods.

I believe most people really underestimate the power of inflation and don't give it full consideration when it comes to their retirement. Keeping up with inflation is one of the most important things you will need to do in retirement, and that will require some careful consideration from you on where to keep your savings and investments. Because if you retire today on a fixed income that doesn't rise to keep up with inflation, eventually you could find yourself going broke.

Inflation and Boiling Frog Syndrome

Inflation is when you pay fifteen dollars for a ten dollar haircut you used to get for five when you had hair.

—SAM EWING

When thinking of inflation, I am reminded of the story of the boiling frog. Not that I would ever do what I am about to say, but the story goes that if you put a frog in boiling water, it will immediately jump out because the water is obviously too hot. But if you put the same frog in cold water and slowly raise the temperature, the frog will just sit there and eventually allow itself to boil. And that is how inflation can get the best of us.

When thinking of inflation, it is important to realize that there are different inflation rates for different products and services. Healthcare and college education, for instance, tend to increase at much higher rates than the consumer price index (CPI) numbers that you often hear the media refer to as our current inflation rate. The CPI is also used by the Social Security Administration to determine if there will be an adjustment in your Social Security benefits.

For individuals thinking of retiring in other parts of the world, you may also want to inquire about the average inflation rate in the country where you would like to retire. While you are at it, you may also want to look at the currency fluctuations compared to the US dollar. If you are going to live in a country in Europe, where the dollar may be weaker than the Euro, you might need to spend more just to keep up with the cost of living in that area, but if you are in a region where the dollar is strong in comparison, such as India, you will get much more buying power for your buck.

For individuals thinking of retiring in other parts of the world, you may also want to inquire about the average inflation rate in the country where you would like to retire.

Just to give you an idea, inflation as measured by CPI in the United States has averaged around 3 to 5 percent over the last twenty to thirty years. This is why many financial planners use 3 to 5 percent as their number when taking inflation into consideration. But if you look at the inflation rate of healthcare, for example, it could be much higher—it could be 8 to 10 percent per year, depending on where you are living.

HURDLE 5–TAXES

People who complain about taxes can be divided into two classes: men and women.

—ANONYMOUS

Now we come to everyone's favorite subject: taxes! Nobody likes to pay taxes, and understandably so, especially when you consider how many different types of taxes we have to pay. Think about all of the different taxes we pay on a regular basis: federal income tax, state tax, Social Security tax, Medicare tax, Medicaid tax, sales tax, luxury tax, property tax, capital gains tax, fuel tax, and so on. The list keeps getting bigger and bigger. Every time we turn around, there is another tax. Sometimes we don't even realize that we are paying some of these taxes. People in high-income tax brackets could be paying way over 50 percent in taxes, depending on their income.

America is a great country, and I can't say that enough. But we are living in interesting times in the United States right now. At the time of writing this book, the credit-card debt held by individuals is over $950 billion, and our national federal deficit is over $19 trillion! Logic suggests that someday we are going to have to pay for this in one way or another, wouldn't you agree?[6]

Imagine a Trillion Dollars

We don't have a trillion-dollar debt because we haven't taxed enough; we have a trillion-dollar debt because we spend too much.

—RONALD REAGAN

If you want to imagine what a trillion dollars looks like in terms of height, imagine this: 100 stacked dollar bills measures .43 inches. The height of 1000 one dollar bills is 4.3 inches. The height of 1 million dollars would be 4,300 inches or 358 feet, which is the height of a 30-40 story building. The height of 1 billion dollars would be 358,510 feet or 67.9 miles. But the height of a trillion dollars would be 67,866 miles. Pretty astounding, huh?[7]

---

6   Robert Harrow, "Average Credit Card Debt in America: 2106 Facts & Figures," Value Penguin, November 28, 2016, https://www.valuepenguin.com/average-credit-card-debt; US Debt Clock, http://www.usdebtclock.org/.

7   "Grasping Large Numbers," The Endowment for Human Development, http://www.ehd.org/science_technology_largenumbers.php.

Now if you want to imagine what a trillion seconds would look like, imagine this. If you counted backward in time, then one million seconds would be less than twelve days ago, one billion seconds would go back to more than thirty-one years ago, and one trillion seconds would take us back to 30,000 BC, give or take a decade or two.

At the time of writing this book in 2017, we have a national deficit of over $19 trillion in the United States that we need to get under control.

If you want to watch an interesting twenty-minute documentary on this subject, check out Tony Robbins's video "The National Debt and Federal Deficit Deconstructed" on YouTube. It will blow your mind! Speaking of Tony Robbins, he recently released his new book, *Money: Master the Game,* which I have to say is one of the best books on finance and money I have ever read. It's worth reading or listening to.

We as a country are living way beyond our means right now, and it is going to be a challenge to get our spending habits back in line. It just seems logical that we will eventually have to pay for this in one way or another. So with this in mind, do you believe our taxes will go up or down in the future? If you are like most people, you probably believe taxes will go up.

Fortunately, there are some very legitimate, legal ways to reduce your tax liabilities, and we will discuss some of those options later in the book.

HURDLE 6–INTEREST RATES

How many millionaires do you know who have become
wealthy by investing in savings accounts? I rest my case.

—ROBERT G. ALLEN

One thing I have noticed in serving our community for the past twenty-five years is that we tend to be savers more than investors. We may be risk takers when it comes to business and entrepreneurship, but when it comes to our savings, we prefer the safety of FDIC-protected bank accounts over other investment options.

I have several clients who have over $1 million in their bank accounts because they are afraid to take risks. And after the 2008 stock-market crash, I can totally understand why. We saw so many people lose over half of their investments in the markets, and the burns from that memory still weigh heavy on our minds.

Many people are more concerned with return *of* their principal than return *on* their principal. They want to make sure their money is going to be safe, and for that reason they are seeking safety and guarantees. I don't think there is anything wrong with that. As Warren Buffett's famous rules to his board at Berkshire Hathaway go: "Rule No. 1: Never Lose Money. Rule No. 2: Never Forget Rule No. 1."

Based on what we just discussed on inflation, the length of your retirement years, and taxes, you need to be aware that keeping all of your money in low-interest-bearing investments may have an adverse effect on the quality of your retirement in the future unless you are very wealthy, have very little in monthly expenses, or have other income sources and are not dependent on the income from your savings for your retirement. Even then, you may still want to get educated on other types of guaranteed products that may yield better returns for you.

I know many in our community also save a significant portion in India because they can get higher interest rates there. On the surface, this seems like a great idea, but when we consider what we have seen over the last few years with regard to the devaluation of the rupee against the dollar, the net effect is often not as beneficial. In addition, there are repatriation rules that one needs to be aware of. But if you are planning on spending your rupees in India while traveling, more power to you!

HURDLE 7–MARKET RISKS

One of the funny things about the stock market is that every time one person buys, another sells, and both think they are astute.

—WILLIAM A. FEATHER

One of the biggest risks to a retiree (and a soon-to-be retiree) is stock-market risk. Imagine for a minute that it is 2008, and you are planning on retiring next month. You have over $1 million in your retirement account when the perfect storm swoops in and all of the markets, including stocks, bonds, and real estate, take a simultaneous tumble and cut the value of your retirement account to $500k.

This changes your retirement picture completely, doesn't it? When you had a million dollars, you may have planned on taking 5 percent withdrawals ($50,000) a year for income. Now that it is at $500,000, you have a decision to make. Will you take the same 5 percent withdrawal for $25,000 a year, take $50,000 a year and risk spending your life savings too rapidly, or keep working until you can make up the shortfall?

This has happened to many people, and it can be devastating. It can be even more devastating if you are already in retirement and you do not have the option to keep working until the market recovers.

The financial-services industry has also realized this, and many investment companies have created new products that can help you protect against such events. Some of these products provide some form of guarantee, with principal protection, guaranteed death benefits, or guaranteed minimum income benefits that can last not only your lifetime but also the lifetime of your spouse. Some of them also give you tax-deferred growth, and others may even include a life-insurance component that may give a tax-free death benefit to your spouse and beneficiaries. We will discuss this further in the upcoming chapters.

As we discussed in this chapter, retirement planning can be likened to climbing Mt. Everest, where the goal is not just to get to the top but also to make it back down safely. We want not only to reach retirement age but also to make it through our retirement years safely. We also learned in this chapter about the seven biggest hurdles in retirement. In the next chapter, I will go over the four biggest lessons I learned from the financial crisis of 2008.

CHAPTER 4

FOUR BIGGEST LESSONS LEARNED FROM THE CRISIS OF 2008

You get recessions, you have stock market declines. If you don't understand that's going to happen, then you're not ready, you won't do well in the markets.

—PETER LYNCH

Do you remember the few years prior to 2008 when the mortgage companies were giving away loans like free candy? "No income, no documentation, no problem," was the slogan we were hearing on television. The interest rates were so low that many people had borrowed almost all of the equity from their homes and were making interest-only payments. Some of them were investing their equities in the stock market, which was soaring at that time.

The home values were going up and up, and many people were in the business of flipping houses. They would buy a home in an area where the prices were soaring, fix it up a little, stage it with nice landscaping, paint, and decorations, and sell it for huge profits. The economy was doing quite well, too, and many people bought homes that not only were overvalued but were also beyond their financial means.

When the crash of 2008 hit, we saw the mortgage and banking industry collapse, and our country was almost ruined. We saw the values of our investment portfolios plummet in value. Our 401(k)s became "201(k)s." Many business owners went bankrupt. Many banks went under. Millions of homeowners ended up upside down in their mortgages, where the amount they owed for their home was greater than the appraised value. During that time, many people lost their homes to foreclosures, and the mortgage and banking industry hasn't been the same since.

I learned some valuable lessons during that time. I watched how some of my clients and friends dealt with all of these massive blows. I also got to see who was the least affected by all this chaos and uncertainty…and who was the most devastated, emotionally as well as financially.

These are the four biggest lessons I learned from the crisis of 2008.

LESSON 1–DEBT: THE GOOD, THE BAD, AND THE UGLY

Too many people spend money they haven't earned, to buy things they don't want, to impress people that they don't like.

—WILL ROGERS

I believe the Indian community has always been pretty mindful when it comes to debt. Even during the crash of 2008, there were very few Indian American-owned hotels that went into foreclosure and fewer Indian American-homeowner defaults. But there are times when we all can get swept away with exuberance.

I remember the people who were the most stressed were the ones who found themselves in huge debt with upside-down mortgages and businesses that were struggling. The people who had little or zero debt were not as fazed. Sure, they were upset that their homes had lost value, but it wasn't a challenge making those mortgage payments.

The way I see it, there is good, bad, and ugly debt. Good debt is used to help you build assets, such as your mortgage or business. Bad debt is like credit-card debt, which just costs you money and is a liability. And ugly debt is debt that is so excessive it snowballs on you and can lead you to bankruptcy and financial devastation.

Lesson 1 is that it is a good idea to keep your debt at a minimum or at least at a manageable level. The reward is peace of mind, which is priceless.

LESSON 2–STAY IN YOUR FINANCIAL REALITY

The thing I have discovered about working with personal finance is that the good news is that it is not rocket science. Personal finance is about 80 percent behavior. It is only about 20 percent head knowledge.

—DAVE RAMSEY

The second lesson I learned from watching the suffering after 2008 was that the people who were the most hurt were the ones who were not staying in their financial reality and capability. It is unreasonable for you to believe that things will always be great, that the price of your home will always be rising, and that you will always have your job. We all know life doesn't work that way. Live beneath your financial means.

I once had an opportunity to interview Jagdish Sheth, a renowned author of many books and professor of marketing at Emory University. At the time, he had just released his book *The Self-Destructive Habits of Good Companies*.

During the interview, I was surprised to learn that one of the top self-destructive habits of businesses is not complacency—it's the undisciplined pursuit of growth! This makes perfect sense when we look in retrospect, especially after we saw some of the largest and strongest companies in the world go bankrupt in the never-ending pursuit of *more*. I am sure you know of business owners in our community who are overleveraging in order to grow their business faster. You probably also know people who strip out the majority of their home equity in an attempt to maximize their returns in the markets.

I am not saying there is anything wrong with that, but I am saying that when things go wrong, which they sometimes will, those folks will be the ones who are the most affected by market downturns.

LESSON 3–UNCERTAINTY IS CERTAIN

Uncertainty is the only certainty there is. And true security is the result of anchoring oneself to the certainty of uncertainty.

—TEAL SWAN

We all know that that there are very few guarantees in the world and that uncertainty is certain. Change is inevitable, and it should be expected.

If we look at the history of the stock market and our world in general, there are always some calamities. Every day, there are a variety of stories in the news about hurricanes, earthquakes, and forest fires, not to mention the man-made afflictions of market crashes, crime, murders, and wars.

I am sure most of you remember the feelings of uncertainty when you first came to this country or started your first business or job. Uncertainty is part of life, and all we can do is be prepared the best we can and be adaptable. Charles Darwin once said that it is not the strongest but the most adaptable that are the fittest.

So the lesson here is that yes, things can happen, but there are steps we can take to plan for those uncertainties. Along these lines, I have an interesting story to share with you in the next chapter on the lessons I learned from my motorcycle accident. I am sure you will find it interesting!

LESSON 4–IT'S A GOOD IDEA TO INSURE A PORTION OF YOUR RETIREMENT

Unless you can watch your stock holding decline
by 50 percent without becoming panic-stricken,
you should not be in the stock market.

—WARREN BUFFETT

The fourth lesson I learned from the crash of 2008 was the importance of protecting a portion of your retirement savings from downside risk. Earlier we saw how some people saw their retirement savings plunge and the possible stress that goes with that.

Since then, many financial planners (myself included) have been recommending that it is not a bad idea to keep 25 to 30 percent of your retirement savings in investments that can provide protection from downside risks. Some of them could be market-linked CDs, which are FDIC insured. You can also use annuities, which offer either a minimum interest rate or a minimum-income benefit. There are also numerous other products that you may consider. To make prudent decisions, you will probably need help from your trusted financial advisor.

They say a cat that is burned by sitting on a hot stove will avoid sitting on a cold stove as well. We all learned a lot about money and ourselves in the crisis of 2008, including lessons on good, bad, and ugly debt, staying within our financial means, the importance of protecting our savings from downside risks, and the uncertainties of life that can sometimes shatter our plans. But does that mean we should not take any risks and sit on the sidelines for the rest of our lives? I don't think so! I believe we need to learn from our mistakes, or as Maya Angelou once said, "When you know better, do better."

CHAPTER 5

SIX INSURANCE QUESTIONS ASKED AFTER MY MOTORCYCLE ACCIDENT

Doesn't "expecting the unexpected" make the unexpected expected?

—GEORGE CARLIN

In the previous chapter, I talked briefly about how uncertain life is. Let me share an interesting story with you. I had a motorcycle accident in the spring of 2016. Yes, that is correct! I am typing this chapter with just one hand, because my other hand is in a splint. I would have to say that if it weren't for my motorcycle clothing and my guardian angels, I might not be here to finish this book.

Let me tell you how it happened. A group of friends and I went riding our bikes through the North Georgia mountains one Saturday. It was a picture-perfect day. We rode for about two and a half hours and stopped to have a nice lunch, and then it was time to make our way back.

A couple that was riding with us needed to get back earlier, so we chose the fastest route back. Before we started, I told the group that I wanted to ride more leisurely and enjoy the ride and that they should not wait for me.

All was going well until a sixteen-year-old boy in a large SUV pulled right in front of me as I was driving at about sixty miles per hour, and due to the size of his vehicle, he blocked both lanes. I couldn't go to the left or the right, and the only option was to slam on the brakes and hope for the best.

It all happened so fast, but I am guessing I laid down my bike trying to avoid hitting him, and my body was thrown across the front of the vehicle to end up on the other side.

Anyway, I remember lying on my back with my arms wide, looking up at the beautiful sky above and wondering if I was dead. I was not scared. In fact, a profound peace had come over me at that time, which is hard to explain.

I could feel my breath, and I wasn't really in a lot of pain at the time, with the exception of my right hand. I could also feel some burns on my left leg from being tossed around on asphalt.

I lay there on the ground until the ambulance came, and after we determined I could move my arms, legs, and neck, they helped me stand up, and the nearby crowd gave me a nice big cheer! I was fortunate enough to be able to walk into the ambulance. Of course, my wife was freaking out when she heard about the accident!

When we got to the hospital, there was a team of six to eight doctors and nurses ready to get to work on me. They had heard that it was a motorcycle accident, so they had to assume the worst. They explained that whenever they have a motorcycle accident, they have to treat it like major trauma and do a full-body CAT scan and X-rays to check for broken bones and other internal damage. I was happy to comply.

I was extremely lucky! I walked away with a dislocated knuckle and fifteen stitches on my right hand, along with some road rash on my legs. But my motorcycle was toast! Looking at the photos of the accident, I noticed that the handlebars and the seat had fallen off. For the sake of the boy and myself, I am truly grateful that the outcome wasn't much worse, as it most certainly could have been.

While lying in the CAT scanner in the emergency room, my thoughts went to my personal finances and insurance benefits. In a close call like an accident, heart attack, or other life-threatening incident, people often find themselves pondering their own well-being, as well as that of their family. Unfortunately, that is not the best time to do insurance planning—it's like planning for homeowners insurance in the middle of a house fire.

Most of us in this country have an ability to manage our risks with proper insurance. We are all required to have liability insurance for our autos to protect the other party in an event that is our fault, and most of us have homeowners insurance to protect our home against fire and other disasters. Even if your mortgage is paid in full, you want to keep the insurance—because why would you want to take a chance on losing your home without proper protection? In general, we insure things that we can't afford to lose, but oftentimes, some of the important things get overlooked.

> *In general, we insure things that we can't afford to lose, but oftentimes, some of the important things get overlooked.*

The following are the six insurance questions that went through my head after the motorcycle accident. I share them with you as my personal assessment so that maybe we can all learn from this unfortunate incident.

QUESTION 1: DO I HAVE ENOUGH LIFE INSURANCE?

Do I really have enough to make sure my family will be taken care of for the rest of their lives? The general rule of thumb is a death benefit of five to ten times your annual salary, but depending on other factors, such as debts and your spouse's ability to work, you might need more. In life insurance, they say, better five years too early than five minutes too late! In retirement planning, you may need additional life insurance to provide replacement of pension income or just additional cushion for your spouse. I'll talk more about the many uses of life insurance later.

And, as a shameless plug, you can also get free, anonymous, term life insurance comparisons on our website at www.ShalinFinancial. com. Our quote engine compares over 175 life insurance companies to help you find the lowest rates. The reason we call it *anonymous* is because you don't have to give out your name and e-mail address to get the quotes. It is free for all to use. But I would highly suggest you talk to us for proper recommendations before making an online application. Okay, back to our regularly scheduled programming.

QUESTION 2: DO I HAVE ADEQUATE DISABILITY INCOME INSURANCE?

A disability income policy provides a monthly income to your family in the event that you are hurt or sick and cannot work for an extended period of time. Let's face it—our lives revolve around our incomes, and when our income stops, so does our lifestyle. That you might be draining your family's finances without being able to contribute as an income producer is a very disturbing thought.

QUESTION 3: AM I COVERED FOR LONG-TERM CARE?

A long-term care policy can help pay for a nurse, assisted-living facility, or home healthcare if you are not able to do daily living activities, such as bathing, eating, and going to the bathroom. For some reason, the Indian American community has been lax with regard to long-term care insurance, but we should all have some game plan in place for our future dignity in old age. We will discuss more about long-term care and the desi community in chapter 10.

QUESTION 4: DO I HAVE ADEQUATE HEALTH INSURANCE?

You would think that would be my first thought, but it wasn't— maybe because I knew I already had a good policy. A good health insurance policy can provide a stop-loss and take care of your major medical bills so that you don't have to go bankrupt. What if the party that was at fault in the accident didn't have any liability insurance? Without a good policy, I would have had to pay all of the medical bills myself. The number-one cause of bankruptcies in the United States is healthcare costs.

QUESTION 5: DO I NEED TO HAVE A LAST WILL AND AN ESTATE PLAN IN PLACE?

We all need some estate plan in place, and at minimum that includes a last will and testament, power of attorneys for healthcare and financial (also known as advanced healthcare directives), and a living will. We will discuss more on basic estate planning in chapter 12.

In 2016, the artist Prince passed away, leaving behind an estate of over $300 million, and it is believed that he didn't have a will and had not done any estate planning. There are chances that over $150 million will go to pay estate taxes, and that's not to mention the potential for family feuds that could go on for years. Imagine what he could've done with all that money if given a choice of paying taxes or supporting a cause of his choice. We will be discussing advanced estate planning in much more detail later in chapters 13 and 14, so stay tuned.

QUESTION 6: WHAT IF THE TABLES WERE TURNED?

I drive a big-ass SUV, too! What if I was the driver and the boy was hurt, paralyzed, or killed due to my negligence? How much compensation would his family want from me? A good auto policy with an umbrella policy that extends the liability coverage of your auto and home would not only provide additional coverage for the party that has been hurt but would also possibly help you with some additional form of asset protection in the event of a lawsuit.

It's not enough to have done the paperwork. You also need to be able to produce the documents to the courts so they can take effect.

After I asked myself these six questions, I realized that even as an insurance agent and financial planner, I had most of the pieces in place—but not the long-term care insurance and the wills. My wife and I had written up our wills and estate plan fifteen years ago, but we didn't know where the papers were.

It's not enough to have done the paperwork. You also need to be able to produce the documents to the courts so they can take effect. For example, if you keep all your important documents in a safe-deposit box, be sure to tell someone where the box is located and make sure they are authorized to open it.

I was telling my friends that this whole motorcycle-accident experience has been like being present at my own funeral. I must have received hundreds of kind and concerned calls and comments from family and friends. You never realize how many people care about you until something like this happens.

A FINAL QUESTION: WILL I RIDE AGAIN?

You can live to be a hundred if you give up all of the things that make you want to live to a hundred.

—WOODY ALLEN

The question I get asked the most now is: "Will you get another motorcycle and ride again?" And I say, "Absolutely!" I realize from experience all of the dangers of riding a motorcycle, but I also know I really like riding and the joy of being with nature on a motorcycle.

Right now, I am grounded by my wife and friends. Before I buy another bike, I would have to get blessings from my wife, kids, and parents because I know firsthand how much assistance is needed just to do the basic things like bathing when one hand is injured, and it is not fair for me to assume they will take care of me in the event of something more serious.

But I do know that I am not the type of person who lives in fear. Accidents can happen anywhere. My family loves snow skiing as well as many water activities, and there are dangers in all of those, too. Interestingly, while I am going to physical therapy, I get to talk to other people who have also been injured. One lady I talked to the other day fell down while standing and broke an arm in two places. Another one cut herself while cooking. So what are you going to do? Not stand, or not cook anymore? I think it is better to have the proper insurance in place for safeguards than to live in fear. It's a universal paradox that we are free to choose, but we are not free from the consequences of our decisions.

CHAPTER 6

OF TIME AND MONEY

*Time is more valuable than money. You can get
more money, but you cannot get more time.*

—JIM ROHN

You may be a seasoned expert in financial concepts or new to some of
the concepts being shared in this book, but before we move forward, I
would like to talk a little about time and money. You can't write a book
on money without talking about the power of compound interest.

THE POWER OF COMPOUND INTEREST

*Compound interest is the eighth wonder of the world. He who
understands it, earns it ... he who doesn't ... pays it!*

—ALBERT EINSTEIN

Most people have heard of compound interest, but for those who haven't, let me explain it to you briefly. With simple interest, if you have one dollar and earned 1 percent per year, in a hundred years you would have $2, because you are earning just 1 percent on that dollar, each year, for a hundred years.

But if you had the compounding effect, where the interest added to your principal also earns interest, you would double your $1 at 1 percent in just seventy-two years.

> **Unfortunately, we have a lot of people who are more focused on accumulating their wealth through addition than growing by multiplication.**

Another way of picturing the compounding effect: You have children, then they have children, and then their children have children. After a while, you have a huge family!

The power of compounding your money is a very powerful thing, and the earlier you start with your savings, the greater its effect will be. Unfortunately, we have a lot of people who are more focused on accumulating their wealth through addition than growing by multiplication. And this brings us to the Rule of 72.

THE RULE OF 72

> *My wealth has come from a combination of living in America, some lucky genes, and compound interest.*
>
> —WARREN BUFFETT

The Rule of 72 is a simple formula that we can use to estimate how long it would take to double your money based on hypothetical interest rates you are receiving. The basic formula is to take the number seventy-two and divide it by your interest rate.

For example, if you are getting a 2 percent interest rate, which many people get today in their bank CDs, just divide seventy-two by two, and you get thirty-six. That is the number of years it would take to double your money! At 4 percent, your money would double every eighteen years. At 6 percent, it would double every twelve years, and at 8 percent, it would double every nine years, and so on.

This rule is useful when you look at your current retirement assets and your current average rate of return and want to estimate the future value of your retirement savings. If you have $250,000 and are averaging 8 percent return, in nine years you should have around $500,000. But if you are earning 2 percent, you are going to need thirty-six years to accomplish the same outcome.

THE RULE OF 72 UPDATED

The Rule of 72 is great for understanding how long it will take to double your money, but it doesn't factor in potential taxes that you might have to pay on your interest earnings along the way. If you are growing your money in bank CDs and other taxable investments, you also have to factor in such taxes.

If you are in a hypothetical combined state and federal tax bracket of, say, 34 percent—with a federal tax rate of 28 percent and a state tax rate of 6 percent—it is going to take an estimated 50 percent longer to double your money when we factor in taxes. Take a CD earning 2 percent, for example, which would have taken thirty-six years to double. When you factor in paying taxes on that 2 percent, your estimated time to double is eighteen years more, for a total of fifty-four years.

If you look at the chart below, you can see how much you would have to earn on a taxable investment in order to equal the earnings on a tax-deferred investment based on various tax brackets and interest rates.

HOW MUCH WOULD YOU HAVE TO EARN EACH YEAR FROM A TAXABLE INVESTMENT IN ORDER TO EQUAL EARNINGS ON A TAX-DEFERRED INVESTMENT?

ANNUAL TAX-DEFERRED YIELD	FEDERAL INCOME TAX BRACKET			
	15%	28%	33%	35%
	ANNUAL TAXABLE EQUIVALENT YIELD			
3%	3.53%	4.17%	4.48%	4.62%
3.5%	4.12%	4.86%	5.22%	5.38%
4%	4.71%	5.56%	5.97%	6.15%
4.5%	5.29%	6.25%	6.72%	6.92%
5%	5.88%	6.94%	7.46%	7.69%
5.5%	6.47%	7.64%	8.21%	8.46%
6%	7.06%	8.33%	8.96%	9.23%
6.5%	7.65%	9.03%	9.70%	10.00%
7%	8.24%	9.72%	10.45%	10.77%
7.5%	8.82%	10.42%	11.19%	11.54%
8%	9.41%	11.11%	11.94%	12.31%
8.5%	10.00%	11.81%	12.69%	13.08%
9%	10.59%	12.50%	13.43%	13.85%
9.5%	11.18%	13.19%	14.18%	14.62%
10%	11.76%	13.89%	14.93%	15.38%

Of course these are all just examples to illustrate a point. You are not going to receive the same interest rate for thirty-six years. Your tax rate is not going to stay the same each year, and you would pay taxes from your income and other sources, so you wouldn't see the reduction on your interest earnings. But it does illustrate the power of taxation on your earnings.

And that is why most financial planners recommend tax-deferred savings vehicles, such as retirement accounts, annuities, and cash value life insurance policies, for their clients when it comes to saving for retirement.

THE POWER OF TAX DEFERRAL AND THE TRIPLE COMPOUNDING OF INTEREST

I was having a conversation with a doctor client of mine about the benefits of tax-deferred compounding, and he said to me, "Rajesh, what difference does it make? It's either screw me now or screw me later when it comes to tax-deferred investments." I explained to him that it *is* a big deal—there is a significant amount of benefit in allowing your money to grow in a tax-deferred account, even if you have to pay the taxes on your growth when you take distributions.

Tax-deferred investments allow you to grow your money faster because you do not have to pay taxes on the interest earnings while you are growing your money, hence causing a triple compounding of interest. You get not only interest on your principal and interest on your interest *but also* interest on your tax savings.

Also, when you do pay taxes at the time of distribution (which may be many, many years in the future), you will also be paying taxes with what we call a *cheaper dollar*, meaning a dollar that is not worth as much because of inflation.

If we compare tax-deferred versus taxable accounts for a $50,000 investment compounding at 8 percent with a 31 percent tax bracket, after thirty years, the amount in the tax-deferred account is $503,140 compared to the taxable account at $250,620. The tax-deferred account shows almost 100 percent more growth over time.

TAX-DEFERRED ACCUMULATION

$100,000 Principal • 8% Compound Interest • 31% Tax Bracket

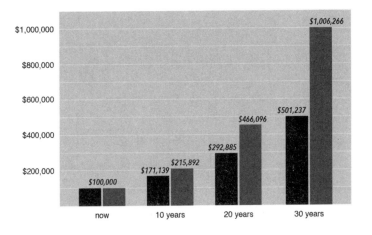

■ Taxable Account
■ Tax-Deferred Account

Consider this: You don't keep your water faucets running in your house all the time, do you? Of course not! You only turn on your faucets when you need water. No one keeps the shower running all the time and jumps in and out without turning off the faucets.

Well then, wouldn't the same strategy be good for your retirement income—to only take out what you need, when you need it, pay the taxes only on the amount that is being distributed, and allow the rest to continue to grow on a tax-deferred basis?

The benefit is that the amount you are not distributing will continue to grow on a tax-deferred basis while minimizing potential tax liabilities.

CHAPTER 7

SAVING FOR RETIREMENT

The question isn't at what age I want to retire, it's at what income.

—GEORGE FOREMAN

We have now discussed most of the challenges of retirement, including longevity, taxes, inflation, having adequate insurance, and market risks. I am sure by now you must have realized the importance of saving for retirement.

But why do some people not save enough for retirement? I don't mean just within the American community but also within the Indian community and everywhere else in the world. It is said that some people will spend more time planning their next vacation than they will their retirement.

Retirement creeps up on us. Think back into your twenties, when you thought you had all the time in the world. You may have thought to yourself, *There is plenty of time to save for retirement! I'll never be this young again—enjoy today!*

Then, in your thirties, you may have gotten married, bought your first house, and started your family. The costs of furnishing your home and childcare expenses took precedence. When you reached your forties, you had to start thinking of your children's college education, which is obviously very important within the Indian household.

Then you got to your fifties, and the thought of preparing for your children's weddings came into the picture. And we all know Indians have epic weddings that can cost a small fortune! Then you find yourself in your sixties and realize, *Holy crap! I didn't save enough for retirement! Why didn't someone tell me to do this earlier?* Does this sound familiar?

THE SURVEY SAID . . .

I mentioned in my introduction that I had conducted a brief financial survey while writing *The Money Talk for Teens* and had reached out to clients and friends from all around the world. I reached out to people in all types of professions, including doctors, lawyers, fellow financial planners, businesspeople, and retirees.

One of the questions I asked in the survey was, "What do you expect from your children in your retirement?" Out of about 150 completed surveys, almost all of them said they really do not expect anything from their children except love, the opportunity to be close to them, and to participate in their lives and the lives of their grandchildren. Most of you believe you will be self-sufficient enough to not want anything from your children except kindness and mutual respect.

WHAT DO YOU EXPECT FROM YOUR CHILDREN IN YOUR RETIREMENT?

I'll be honest with you—I was a little teary-eyed reading those responses! You could feel the love the parents had for their children. Based on those answers (if those are your intentions as well), wouldn't it make sense to make sure that you really are self-sufficient enough to climb the mountain of retirement and leap over the seven biggest hurdles in retirement we talked about earlier?

We have enough tools in retirement planning to help you do this. You just need to take the time to become educated on your options and act accordingly. I believe that one of the best things you can do for yourself and your retirement plan is take advantage of individual retirement accounts (IRAs) and qualified business retirement plans, which are often available from your employer. If you own your own business, it may be worth considering starting a company retirement plan to help your employees prepare for their retirement years also.

AUTOMATE YOUR RETIREMENT PLAN

The best time to start thinking about your
retirement is before the boss does.

—ANONYMOUS

I have found that the best way to save for retirement is to automate it. What I mean by that is to set up an automatic monthly withdrawal from your checking account into your retirement account. If you are fortunate enough to have a 401(k) at work, go ahead and contribute as much as you can. See if you can max out your contributions each year. If you can't max out, see if you can commit to putting aside at least 10 to 20 percent of your income toward your retirement. The earlier you start, the more time you will have for compounding to take effect. You probably won't miss that income much after a while, and you will be taking a huge step for your future. It is amazing how consistent, small amounts contributed on a monthly basis and combined with the power of compound interest and tax-deferred growth can add up over time.

If you are a business owner, you are really fortunate! You have many different types of retirement plans that you can choose from, including 401(k) plans, SIMPLE 401(k) plans, SEP IRA plans, profit sharing plans, and defined benefit plans. Some of these plans allow you to contribute a significant amount of your income each year and also allow you to take a tax deduction for your contributions. You will probably need assistance in choosing the right plan based on the size of your company and the amount you would like to contribute on a yearly basis. But once it is set up, you too are ready to automate. You will also be helping your employees if you have a plan for their retirement.

I realize that in some industries, such as fast-food restaurants, hotels, and other small businesses, it is difficult to get the employees to participate because of high turnover, lower income scales, and the costs associated with employer contributions. If you are a business owner, you will need to look at IRAs, annuities, and possibly life insurance as your retirement saving vehicles. We will talk about the benefits of annuities and life insurance shortly.

RETIREMENT PLANS FOR HIGH-INCOME EARNERS

*A fine is a tax for doing something wrong. A
tax is a fine for doing something right.*

—ANONYMOUS

We have many doctors, software consultants, and other professionals in our community who many times are solopreneurs and are blessed with high incomes. I have quite a few clients who have incomes in excess of $500,000 to $1 million a year. If you have a similar income in addition to the traditional business retirement plans, you may want to look at defined benefit plans which, depending on your age and income, will allow you to contribute significantly more than the traditional 401(k) and profit sharing plans. I have seen people over age fifty able to contribute several hundred thousand dollars per year into their retirement plans and also take a deduction on those contributions.

For high-income earners, there are many advanced planning strategies to implement to help both minimize your taxes and give back to the community in a variety of ways. Unfortunately, the in-depth details of these strategies are beyond the scope of this book. You can reach out to qualified financial planners for help in finding some of these solutions, based on your personal desires and situations.

THE DOWNSIDE OF QUALIFIED RETIREMENT PLANS

For those of you who don't know the difference between a qualified retirement plan and a nonqualified plan, qualified retirement plans allow you to take a tax deduction at the time of contribution, whereas nonqualified plans may be taxable (depending on what investments are part of the plan). Most employer-based retirement plans are qualified retirement plans.

Many benefits of qualified retirement plans are mentioned previously, including possible tax deductions, tax-deferred growth on your savings, the ability to dollar-cost average into various investments on a monthly basis, and in many cases, protection from lawsuits and bankruptcies (retirement plans are protected from those events in some states).

So what could be some of the downsides of these plans? Well, for some people, a possible downside could be that their contributions may be limited because they are highly compensated, particularly in some types of businesses, such as hotels and convenience stores.

The reason for this limitation is that traditional 401(k) plans have different tests that have to be done to make sure the plan isn't just benefiting the owners and highly compensated employees. Not to get into too many complicated details on the different tests, but if the employer plan doesn't involve enough of the lower-compensated employees, the highly compensated employees are limited in how much they can contribute. So, many times, the owners try to contribute the maximum allowable, and at the end of the year they get a check back from the 401(k) company telling them that they have overcontributed to their plan based on the average compensation test and the average deferral test.

In industries like hotels and fast food, as well as other small businesses where the employees are paid near the minimum wage, the employees are reluctant or unable to contribute, making it difficult for the owners to contribute.

There are ways to get around these situations by establishing a safe harbor 401(k) or a SIMPLE 401(k), but the employer would have to commit to contributing at least 2 to 3 percent of the employees' wages to avoid the annual testing requirements. This may not be a problem if you only have a few employees and their salaries are not very high, but if you have many employees and the annual payroll is huge, it could make this type of plan unaffordable to the employer.

There are many types of employer-sponsored retirement plans, including SEP IRAs, SIMPLE 401(k) plans, profit sharing plans, and several types of defined benefit plans. The rules in some of these plans may be a little confusing, so I am not going to go into all of your options, but I will say that it would be worth your while to explore your options with a qualified financial planner.

THE CHALLENGES OF HAVING TOO MUCH MONEY IN RETIREMENT PLANS

There are some people who have been smart and blessed and have contributed a lot of money into their retirement plans over the years, and their retirement plans have done exceedingly well. Most of the time these people are high-income earners such as doctors, software engineers, and other professionals who have been contributing large sums of money in their plans for many years and have also gotten impressive returns, resulting in multiple millions of dollars in their retirement accounts. I have several clients who have in excess of $3–5 million in their qualified retirement accounts. Some of them are in their early fifties. Most are very simple, low-key desi folk who have zero debt, spend very little money, and live happy, simple lives. You gotta love them!

Now, imagine the future value of these accounts when we apply the Rule of 72, as discussed in the previous chapter. Let's take a hypothetical example. With an average 8 percent annual return on the investments over time, a $5 million account will be worth approximately $10 million in nine years and an estimated $20 million in eighteen years.

You may be thinking, *Wow, what a nice position to be in!* And it certainly is, in terms of wealth accumulation. The challenge comes in the wealth-distribution phase, when these folks are ready to transfer the wealth to their heirs. The challenge they have is that at some time in the future, they or their heirs will have to pay taxes on the distributions. Unfortunately, there aren't a whole lot of options to avoid those taxes—with the exception of charitable giving.

And if these people's total estates are over the estate tax limits of that time, they will also have to pay estate taxes on those assets as they transfer them to their children and grandchildren. The current estate tax limit in 2017 is $5,490,000 per individual; these limits change each year and are indexed for inflation.[8] When we combine the income taxes and estate taxes that would be attributed to their retirement plans, we could be looking at more than 70 percent of the retirement assets subject to taxes. No doubt it's a high-class problem to have, but it is still a problem.

There are solutions for people in these situations, too. Consider some charitable giving with your retirement accounts and possibly taking earlier distributions to purchase a life insurance policy, which not only can provide a much more efficient wealth-transfer option but also may provide liquidity to help pay for estate taxes. If you are one of the fortunate ones in this position, you should meet with qualified financial and estate tax planners and look at your options.

One thing I have learned over the last twenty-five years in the financial-services industry and in life in general is that there are pros and cons to just about everything. For most of us, qualified retirement plans are an excellent way to take tax deductions each year and stock up a bunch of money for retirement, which we will probably need, based on life expectancies and future inflation rates.

But there are times that even a good thing can turn bad, as in the previous example of retirement accounts that have grown to multiple millions of dollars. Unfortunately, it is not viable for many small

---

8   "What's New? – Estate and Gift Tax," IRS, October 28, 2016, https://www.irs.gov/businesses/small-businesses-self-employed/estate-tax.

businesses to establish qualified retirement plans because of the costs and rules associated with them.

There is, however, another solution that can provide tax-deferred growth, tax-free death benefit, and possibly tax-free withdrawals: *permanent life insurance.* This gives us a nice segue to talk about life insurance, so let's get started.

CHAPTER 8

THE ULTIMATE RETIREMENT PLAN

Money can't buy happiness, but it certainly is a stress reliever.

—BESA KOSOVA

There is an old saying that if the only tool you have in your toolbox is a hammer, everything starts to look like a nail. I would like to ask you in advance to excuse my exuberance over the next couple of chapters while we discuss life insurance and annuities because even though I have many financial tools in my toolbox, these two get me a little excited. Perhaps it's because I started my financial-services career on the life insurance side and understand the many uses and benefits quite well. My intention is just to share the pros and cons of these products and how they may be able to help you in your financial planning goals, as there is a lot of conflicting information floating around on the Internet.

SURVEY: WHAT IS THE MOST IMPORTANT THING YOU LOOK FOR IN AN INVESTMENT PRODUCT?

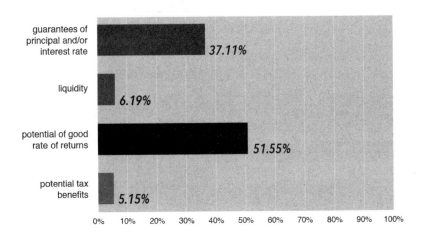

I started my career in the financial-services industry back in 1991 with New York Life. It was and still is a great company. They provided us with excellent training, and I learned a lot about the benefits and the many uses of life insurance. But after a while, I couldn't see myself representing just one company and wanted more flexibility to be able to offer a variety of products, including many different types of life insurance, health insurance, stocks, bonds, and a variety of investment products, so I left the company to start my own brokerage operation.

Over the years, I have had the opportunity to serve thousands of individuals and business owners for their insurance-planning needs, and I've done so in an ever-changing industry where there is always something new to be learned.

Last year I did a webinar on "The Many Faces of Life Insurance," which was very well-received by our community. You are welcome to watch the replay on our website at www.RajeshJyotishi.com.

Life insurance in this country has really evolved over the last several decades. We have more options for life insurance than ever before. It used to be that we had only two options for life insurance: either basic term insurance or whole life. The term policies were also very basic and did not offer long-term rate guarantees.

Today we have a large variety of term life policies that can offer rate guarantees from five years all the way up to age 120. We have technology that allows us to compare hundreds of policies instantly to find the lowest rates. Some companies even offer return-of-premium term life insurance, where after the term period, if there has been no death, you have an option to get all of your premiums you have paid into the policy returned to you.

In the permanent life insurance space, we have options for whole life, universal life, variable life, and the newly popular indexed universal life. In my opinion, they all have their pros and cons, depending on your needs and objectives. Generally speaking, most of you should consider a permanent life insurance policy if you plan to keep your policy for your entire life, even if you live to age 120, and we do have policies that will cover you that long.

I won't go into too much detail on these policies here, because it can be confusing. But I *do* want to talk a little about some of the benefits of life insurance, as well as some of the most common applications.

THE THREE UNIQUE TAX BENEFITS OF LIFE INSURANCE

Life insurance is funny! You bet you are going to die, they bet you are going to live. You invest a lot of money and hope they win.

—ANONYMOUS

Some of the most appealing aspects of life insurance are its tax benefits. The first is that the death benefit is generally income tax-free. This is true for term life as well as cash value life policies, which allows us to accumulate a vast amount of wealth in a tax-free wealth-transfer vehicle. The second benefit, primarily in cash-value type policies, is that the money grows tax-deferred, just like with qualified retirement accounts. This means that you have the ability to accumulate enormous amounts of wealth without having to pay taxes on interest and dividends.

The third, very useful benefit of cash value policies is the ability to borrow against the cash value built up inside the policy, allowing you to take tax-free withdrawals that can be used for a variety of purposes, including supplementing your retirement, funding your children's college education, or any other purpose you can think of.

These three very attractive benefits make cash value policies very popular with people who understand them. Compare this to the retirement accounts we previously discussed, where there are limits on how much you can contribute and you have to pay taxes upon distribution. Traditional and Roth IRAs have annual limits, currently in 2017 of $5,500 per person, or $6,500 if you are age fifty or older.[9] The qualified retirement plans that we discussed in the

9   "Retirement Topics – IRA Contribution Limits" IRS, November 21, 2016, https://www.irs.gov/retirement-plans/plan-participant-employee/retirement-topics-ira-contribution-limits.

previous chapters have various and larger limits, but as we discussed, not everyone's circumstances allow him or her to take advantage of these plans. But with a life insurance policy, your limits and flexibility are much greater. The only real limits of contributions are your insurability, what you can afford, and financial underwriting that has to justify your reasons to purchase larger life policies.

The only tax caveat is that you generally cannot deduct life insurance premiums. Business owners may deduct only $50,000 of basic term life insurance costs for themselves and their employees, but if you deduct the premiums, the death benefit becomes taxable, and why would you want to deduct the smaller premium and have to pay taxes on the much larger death benefit? (However, there are numerous advanced planning strategies that allow us to pay taxes on just the insurance costs and allow the cash value to grow on a tax-deferred basis.)

Permanent life insurance policies are an excellent option for people who are looking for the most efficient way to accumulate and transfer wealth. When we utilize irrevocable life insurance trusts (ILITs) or other corporate structures to hold and fund the life insurance policies, it also allows us to transfer the wealth not only income tax-free but also estate tax-free! That is why life insurance is the preferred financial-planning vehicle in estate planning to transfer wealth and provide liquidity to pay for estate taxes.

The benefit of term life insurance is that most of the time, it is very affordable and allows you to have a significant amount of life insurance at very low cost while you are raising your family. The downside is that most people purchase term life policies with twenty-year or thirty-year rate guarantees, and once the rate guarantee is over, the premiums skyrocket and you have to go through medical underwriting to qualify for lower rates—and if you have health issues, such as diabetes or high blood pressure, it may not be possible to qualify for preferred rates. In many cases, it is not possible to qualify for any coverage, depending on your health.

My recommendation for some people is to have both term and permanent policies—a large term policy that provides a greater death benefit while raising your family and a permanent cash value policy that can serve as your wealth-accumulation and transfer tool. Of course, make sure you are in your affordability range, as permanent life policies are a commitment.

MANY APPLICATIONS OF LIFE INSURANCE

Fun is like life insurance; the older you get, the more it costs.

—FRANK MCKINNEY HUBBARD

You have a lot of choices, and there are many applications of life insurance that you may not have considered. Some of the applications of life insurance include:

- **Income replacement:** The most widely used application for life insurance is income replacement. If you die while you are raising your family, the death benefit from your life insurance policy can help your family replace your income while they adjust to their lives without you. A general rule in life insurance as income replacement is that you should have a death benefit of about five to ten times your annual salary. The target amount can vary based on the amount of debt you have, whether your spouse works, and how well-off you would like to leave your family.

- **Retirement-plan supplement:** You can use cash value life insurance to supplement your retirement income.

- **Pension maximization:** If you retire from a company and have a choice of taking a pension that pays, for example, $2,000 a month for the rest of your life or one that pays $1,500 a month for joint life between you and your spouse, consider taking the $2,000 a month option and purchasing a life insurance policy with the extra $500 to provide an income replacement for your spouse. Just make sure you qualify for the policy before making the decision.

- **Estate planning:** If your estate is over the exemption amounts, you may have an estate tax liability. Consider purchasing a second-to-die (survivor) life insurance policy, which pays after the second spouse's death to provide the necessary liquidity to pay for the estate taxes. We'll cover this more in the estate-planning section (chapters 13 and 14).

- **Buy/sell agreements:** Let's say you have a business with business partners. What happens if one of the partners passes away? Now you may be stuck with your partner's spouse or other family member as your new partner, and he or she may not be able to contribute to the business in the same way as your partner. A buy/sell agreement funded with life insurance provides business partners liquidity to buy out each other's partnership shares in the event of a death.

- **Charitable giving:** If you want to leave a gift to your favorite charitable cause, life insurance is used quite often in charitable giving. You can designate a portion (or all) of your death benefit to the organization of your choice.

There are also advanced charitable-giving strategies you can employ that may give you additional tax benefits.

- **Wealth-replacement vehicle:** Many times, people use life insurance as a wealth-replacement vehicle when making a large charitable donation. The life insurance policy is used to replace the large donation made to a charity so the children do not feel left out. For example, you donated one million dollars of a stock and then bought a million-dollar life insurance policy to replace the wealth that was given away. We'll talk a little more on this in chapter 15, Leaving a Charitable Legacy.

- **Life insurance/long-term care policies:** We now have life insurance policies that can provide optional long-term care benefits.

Case Study

Mr. and Mrs. Patel own several hotels and do not have a company retirement plan because of the restrictions and expenses associated with them. They have traditional IRAs and have maxed out the allowable contributions for years. They would like to save for retirement, but they also believe their hotels will provide them with retirement income for life and may not need to access those funds.

The Patel's financial advisor recommended that they purchase permanent life insurance policies such as whole life or indexed universal life and max fund the policies to allow for maximum cash accumulation. By doing so, the Patels will have additional funds in their policies that could be used to supplement their retirement. If they don't need to use those funds, the funds will pass to their children and grandchildren as a tax-free death benefit. In the Patel's case, they may also be able to use their policies as collateral assignment for future loans.

SELLING YOUR LIFE INSURANCE POLICIES

There are times when people find that their life insurance policies are unaffordable and decide to surrender them to take out any cash value, or just let them lapse by not paying any more premiums. This could happen when people no longer want, need, or can afford their policies. Some people may have purchased a survivorship life insurance policy when the estate tax exemptions were $600,000, and now that they are over $5,490,000, the need for the survivorship policy is no longer there.

There is another solution for people who want to get rid of their existing life policies but would like to get something more in return: viatical settlements. This solution is typically for people who are over age sixty-five and in poor health. Viatical settlements basically involve selling your life insurance policy to a company that would pay you a portion of your death benefit and take over as the new owner and beneficiary of your policy. They would continue making the payments on your policy until your death and hope to profit over time.

Viatical settlements can be done on a variety of life insurance policies, including universal life, survivorship life, and term life that is still convertible to a permanent policy. Here is a case study on how this may work.

Case Study

Mr. Bedi is seventy-five years old and in frail health. He purchased a $2 million universal life policy in the 1980s, when he owned his business, for the purpose of protecting his company and family. His premiums are currently $36,000 per year, and the cash surrender value is just $3,700—not enough to cover the money invested in the policy—and the premiums are not affordable for him and his family.

Even though his health is frail, he could conceivably live for many more years, and his family just doesn't have the funds to pay for his life insurance premiums. He and his family decided to sell his policy to a viatical settlement company, and they received around $259,000 rather than letting his policy lapse and receiving nothing. They were able to use the money received from the sale of Mr. Bedi's policy to pay for his healthcare expenses and also make sure he and Mrs. Bedi can enjoy the final years of their lives.

The money received from viatical settlements is taxable—unlike the death benefit of life insurance, which is generally federal income tax-free—but it is a good alternative for some people that may be worth considering.

BUYER BEWARE!

As you can tell, there are many uses and applications for life insurance in financial planning, and as I said in the introduction of this chapter, it is easy to think we should use life insurance for everything, including retirement planning, college-education funding, estate planning, charitable giving, and many other applications.

There are pros and cons to everything, and it is important to understand all of your options with life insurance as well as the alternatives that are available to you. There are many financial tools available—you just need to make sure you are working with a skilled craftsperson who knows how to use them appropriately.

CHAPTER 9

PLANNING FOR RETIREMENT INCOME

Lack of money is the root of all evil.

—GEORGE BERNARD SHAW

As a financial planner, one of the biggest questions I get asked about retirement is, "How much money will I need to have for retirement?" This is a great question. Because the answer can depend on many variables, such as "Where you are going to live?" "What will cost of living be there?" and "What type of lifestyle do you plan on leading?"

But I would suggest that an *even better* question might be, "How much income do you want to have in retirement?" Because it is our income that dictates the type of lifestyle we lead, isn't it?

You can have millions of dollars in assets tied up in land, homes, businesses, jewelry, farms, and many other things, but unless those things produce income, they are just assets. They may look great on your net-worth statement, but they may not do much to enhance the quality of your day-to-day life.

I have several computer-consultant clients who have hundreds of employees, and their businesses may be worth several million dollars, but the owners don't feel very wealthy. All they know is that they have a huge payroll that must be met each month and that their personal lifestyle often lacks the fullness of abundance.

Here is another example for you. Have you ever been out of work, where you were between jobs and your income had stopped? Do you remember how it totally changed your perception of how much money you could spend? You could have a hundred thousand dollars in your savings, but the thought of having to spend down your savings to support your lifestyle probably made you uncomfortable, didn't it? I know it did for me!

This also happens to us in retirement. We don't like to spend our principal unless we have to. We want to live off our interest or income, and that makes us feel like we are staying within our means. Spending our principal makes us feel like we are going broke, which could be true in some ways. And that is why I believe that retirement planning is more about income planning. Of course, we also need our assets, which we can use as income generators.

THE FIVE-MINUTE RETIREMENT PLAN

If we command our wealth, we shall be rich and free.
If our wealth commands us, we are poor indeed.

—EDMUND BURKE

There are several ways to calculate the amount of retirement assets you will need. One way is to do an in-depth analysis, taking into consideration all of your possible income sources for retirement, including your retirement accounts, pension plans, annuities, rental property, Social Security benefits, and possible earnings from a job or business (if you are planning on working during your retirement years).

Most retirement accounts, such as IRAs and company-sponsored plans like 401(k)s, require you to wait until after age fifty-nine and a half before being able to take distributions without a tax penalty. Social Security benefits may begin at age sixty-two for some people but with reductions of benefits for earlier withdrawals.

Or you could use what we call the *4 percent withdrawal rule to calculate your retirement-asset needs*. Bill Bengen, a financial planner from California, created this rule about twenty years ago.

Basically, what the 4 percent withdrawal rule states is that if you invested your savings reasonably into a well-diversified portfolio and withdrew 4 percent for income, based on multiple possibilities of the ups and downs in the markets, the probability of running out of your money during your lifetime becomes lesser than withdrawing a higher percentage on a regular basis. Of course, this is just a rule of thumb and is not guaranteed, but it does give us a way to come up with a quick calculation.

Ideally, you would want to earn more than 4 percent on your portfolio so that the value of your portfolio would increase over time, allowing you to keep up with inflation. If you recall from our section on inflation, the value of our dollar diminishes with time and the amount of income you need will rise along with the cost of living.

So think about it for a minute. What is your magic number? In today's dollars, how much gross income would you like to have in order to live your ideal retirement lifestyle?

SURVEY: DO YOU KNOW HOW MUCH YOU NEED FOR RETIREMENT?

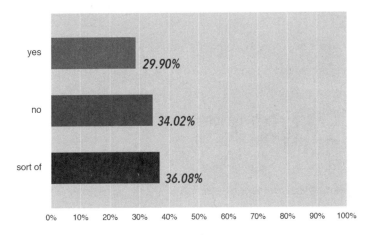

If you were to say, "My magic number is $40,000 a year," then based on the 4 percent withdrawal rule and without factoring in Social Security or any other income sources, you would need $1 million in retirement assets. If you were to say, "My magic number is $80,000 per year," then you would need $2 million.

But what if you were to withdraw at 5 percent, 6 percent, or 7 percent? Numbers and outcomes can change pretty dramatically, can't they? If you are withdrawing 6 percent from $1 million, you are making $60,000 a year compared to $40,000. That is a significant difference in income. At the same time, this could also increase the risk of running out of your funds depending upon market returns.

Once we have your ideal retirement-income number, we can work to find out what the future value of that will be based on a hypothetical inflation rate. We can also get an estimate from the

Social Security department on how much retirement benefit you may be entitled to during retirement. Social Security benefits can also vary based on if you choose to take benefits earlier or wait until you reach full retirement age. To find out what your Social Security benefits are, you can go to www.ssa.gov.

HOW TO GENERATE A GUARANTEED INCOME FOR LIFE

It's a recession when your neighbor loses his job;
it's a depression when you lose your own.

—HARRY TRUMAN

From my experience, our community tends to be pretty conservative when it comes to investing. It seems that whenever I am talking with anyone about making various investments, one of the first questions they ask is if the returns are guaranteed. Unfortunately, most things—such as stocks, bonds, mutual funds, and alternative investments—are not guaranteed. In order to find guarantees, we have to look at FDIC-insured bank accounts (where the interest rates have been pretty low over the last decade) or some forms of insurance products such as annuities.

WHAT IS AN ANNUITY?

For those of you who do not know what annuities are, let me explain. Annuities have been around for a very long time. Annuities came to America in 1759 in the form of a retirement pool for church pastors. They were funded by the church leaders and the congregation to provide a lifetime stream of income to ministers and their families.

Annuities were also a way many people saved for retirement before individual retirement accounts were introduced in 1974.[10]

An annuity, simply put, is a contract between you and a third party, which is usually an insurance company. You make either lump sum or periodic payments over time and in return have an option to get a stream for either a lifetime or for a certain number of years.

Some other examples of annuities are lottery winners, who often choose to get a certain amount of money for life rather than a one-time lump sum. A pension plan could also be considered a form of an annuity because it provides a stream of income for your and your spouse's lifetimes. Many sports figures also choose to take their income in annuity form rather than lump sum. This can help them spread out their incomes over time and also keeps them from squandering their earnings. In your case, the annuities are sold by insurance companies and designed to do these three main things:

1. Provide a vehicle to grow your money on a tax-deferred basis like retirement accounts.

2. Provide you with multiple ways to take income distributions when you are ready (usually, after age fifty-nine and a half).

3. Provide a death benefit that can be passed on to your beneficiaries.

Some of the modern annuities also offer additional living benefits such as long-term care benefits, life insurance riders, as well as guaranteed minimum income or withdrawal benefits.

Just as we discussed with regard to life insurance in chapter 8, the annuity landscape has changed significantly over the last several decades. Today you can purchase many different types of annuities.

---

10   Mark P. Cussen, "Introduction to Annuities," Investopedia, http://www.investo-pedia.com/university/annuities/.

Annuities are used primarily for retirement savings and have similar features to retirement accounts. One of the key benefits of annuities is the ability to contribute unlimited amounts of money into them and grow money on a tax-deferred basis. Although you cannot deduct the contributions as you can in an IRA or 401(k), you can invest a significant portion of your savings and grow them on a tax-deferred basis for retirement.

There are many different types of annuities. Fixed annuities give a stated interest rate like a bank CD but on a tax-deferred basis. Variable annuities offer a selection of mutual fund subaccounts that you can choose from. Indexed annuities offer returns based on the performance of certain indexes, such as the S&P 500 and Dow Jones.

WHY ANNUITIES HAVE A BAD REPUTATION

If you have ever listened to some talk-show hosts, you may have heard them bash annuities. Some of the criticisms are quite reasonable. I believe that the three main reasons talk show hosts hate annuities are that annuities are too expensive, they are too complex, and they can lock you in and are sometimes difficult to get out of.

There is some validity to all of their concerns, but I don't believe these three concerns make all annuity products inherently bad. Just as there are good and bad versions of just about all financial products, annuities have their pros and cons. But in the right circumstances, they can be the perfect fit. It is up to us to take the time to understand what we are getting into before signing on the dotted line. There are some significant benefits of annuities for retirees, which are as follows.

SOME OF THE MOST COMMON BENEFITS OF ANNUITIES

While money can't buy happiness, it certainly
lets you choose your own form of misery.

—GROUCHO MARX

Tax-deferred growth: All of your money grows tax-deferred, which allows you to minimize your taxes while accumulating wealth and may also help you reduce the taxation of your interest and Social Security earnings in retirement. As you may know, we have to pay taxes on interest earnings, capital gains, and dividends. Because annuities allow you to grow your money on a tax-deferred basis, you do not have to pay taxes until you take distributions.

Your interest earnings may also put you in a category where you have to pay taxes on your Social Security earnings. The following is a passage from the Social Security Administration website.

Some people have to pay federal income taxes on their Social Security benefits. This usually happens only if you have other substantial income (such as wages, self-employment, interest, dividends, and other taxable income that must be reported on your tax return) in addition to your benefits.

No one pays federal income tax on more than 85 percent of his or her Social Security benefits based on Internal Revenue Service (IRS) rules. If you:

- **file a federal tax return as an "individual"** and your *combined income* is

- □ between $25,000 and $34,000, you may have to pay income tax on up to 50 percent of your benefits.

- □ more than $34,000, up to 85 percent of your benefits may be taxable.

- **file a joint return**, and you and your spouse have a *combined income* that is

  - □ between $32,000 and $44,000, you may have to pay income tax on up to 50 percent of your benefits

  - □ more than $44,000, up to 85 percent of your benefits may be taxable.

- **are married and file a separate tax return**, you probably will pay taxes on your benefits.

Because annuity income is tax-deferred until distribution, it can also help you reduce current income taxes as well as those on your Social Security earnings. For more information, please visit ssa.gov.

No contribution limits by the IRS: There are no contribution limits in nonqualified annuities, allowing you to contribute as much as you want. The only limits will be the ones set by insurance companies on how much they are willing to accept from a single investor.

I have had several clients who have invested as much as a million dollars at a time in annuities.

Avoids probate: Annuities are transferred to your beneficiaries by beneficiary designations—just like life insurance policies and other retirement accounts—and are not subject to the hassles of probate. They also cannot be contested, whereas your will can.

We will go over probate and the four ways to transfer property in the estate-planning section (chapters 13 and 14), but basically, beneficiary designations make it easier to transfer assets from one person to another in a way that cannot easily be contested by other people.

Asset protection and creditor protection (in some states): Annuities and cash value life insurance policies may provide protection from lawsuits and creditors. The rules vary state by state. To find out more about your state's rules, visit www.AssetProtectionSociety.com.

Protection from Medicaid spend down: Some annuities also offer the ability to shelter your assets from a possible Medicaid spend down. A Medicaid spend down is when you are trying to qualify for Medicaid but are not eligible because you have too many assets and must spend down those assets for your healthcare needs in order to qualify.

LIVING BENEFITS OF MODERN-DAY ANNUITIES

Some of today's annuities offer additional living benefits, some of which I list here. These benefits are very attractive to retirees who are looking for guarantees of lifetime income, guaranteed death benefits, or some form of principal protection. Please keep in mind that some of these extra benefits may have additional charges associated with them and that the guarantees mentioned are guarantees from the underlying insurance company and are subject to the claims-paying abilities of that insurance company.

Guaranteed minimum income: Some annuities today allow you to create a pension-like guaranteed income for life. Some of them, which are tied to stock markets or indexes, also allow step-ups on account values, allowing you to increase your income amounts as the underlying account values rise.

Guaranteed minimum interest rate credits: Some variable and indexed annuities offer a minimum interest rate for a given number of years. For example, you might be guaranteed 6 percent credit to your income benefit base for ten years. If the stock market performs better than the 6 percent, your account is credited by that amount; otherwise, you have 6 percent increases to look forward to. Please note, the interest credits are usually applied to your income base which may be different than the actual account and surrender values based on market performances.

Downside stock market protection: Some indexes and variable annuities whose returns are tied to stock-market performance also offer protection from market declines but still offer upside potential. This is often an attractive feature over a fixed annuity, which gives a fixed interest rate in a low interest rate environment.

Guaranteed death benefit: This is also a valuable feature. Let's say you invested $250,000 in your account, the stock market crashes, the value of your account drops to $200,000, and then you die. Your spouse or beneficiary will get the $250,000 as a guaranteed death benefit. Some annuities also offer the guaranteed death benefit as an optional life insurance rider, which are tax-free and stay level even after you have started your distributions. This could be valuable for someone who is not insurable for life insurance.

Long-term care benefits: We are starting to see annuities that offer long-term care withdrawal benefits to help pay for costs associated with home healthcare, nursing homes, and assisted-living facilities.

These and other features of annuities are what make annuities desirable to many who are risk averse and are looking for guarantees of some sort. As you can tell, when we add some of these features it can get complicated, and the underlying costs may also rise accordingly, affecting the overall market performance of the annuity. But for people who want guarantees with their investments, annuities offer a wide variety.

Case Study 1

Mr. Krishna is a very conservative investor. He mostly keeps his savings in bank CDs with a five-year holding period for slightly higher interest rates. His CD was about to mature, and the new rate being offered for a five-year CD was 2 percent. He was able to find a fixed annuity that gives a 3.1 percent rate guarantee for five years. The annuity will also give him tax-deferred growth on his savings without any stock-market volatility.

Fixed annuities are very similar to bank CDs in that they often offer a fixed interest rate for a specified number of years. Some fixed annuities offer a higher rate for the first couple of years and a lower rate for the remainder of the term. Fixed annuities are also relatively easy to shop for. There are many websites that allow you to compare fixed annuity rates. Of course, your insurance agent or broker may also be able to assist you with that. Keep in mind that if you wish, once your rate guarantee period is over, you may transfer your annuity to a new company or product that may offer a better rate for you, similar to finding CDs with higher rates. Please be aware of any applicable surrender charges from the insurance companies.

Case Study 2

Mr. and Mrs. Gandhi have had a fixed annuity for many years, which they purchased when the interest rates were higher. Now that the interest rates have dropped, they are looking for alternative solutions. Their financial advisor showed them an indexed annuity, which, like a fixed annuity, also offers guarantees on their principal but bases its returns on how the underlying stock-market indexes perform over time.

The new annuity product also offers optional riders that can provide a minimum interest rate and a lifetime income benefit. After much consideration, the Gandhis transferred their annuity into the new product for the potential of higher returns and for the guaranteed lifetime incomes. The pros of this decision are that it may be possible for the Gandhis to have a higher rate over time and a guaranteed minimum income option when they are ready to take distributions. The cons are that they will have a new surrender charge from the annuity company for several years, and they do not know exactly what type of returns they will achieve over time.

ANNUITIES AND THE TIME I GOT SUED

> *When a person tells you that you hurt them,*
> *you don't get to decide that you didn't.*
>
> —LOUIS C.K.

When I was taking my financial-planning course at Oglethorpe University in Atlanta, the instructors said something that was a little scary. They said that in the financial services, it's not a matter of *if* but of *when* you will get sued for something or other.

Of course I just shrugged it off because those types of things only happen to other people, right? Just like motorcycle accidents only happen to other people. Well, unfortunately, both the motorcycle accident and the lawsuit happened to me.

I had clients who, in 2005, invested $100,000 into a variable annuity that offered guaranteed income benefits, but they misunderstood how the benefits worked. In 2008, when the stock markets collapsed, the value of their underlying annuity dropped to around $80,000, and they wanted to take all of their money out of the annuity, including the interest credits. Unfortunately, that is not the way the product worked.

So they filed a complaint against me in which FINRA (Financial Industry Regulatory Authority) reviewed the complaint and found no wrongdoing. The clients couldn't find any attorneys to take their case because the case was not only too small but also difficult to prove. Somehow, they stumbled on a pro bono law school in California that took their case to give the law students experience.

At that time, I had also changed broker/dealer, and my previous broker/dealer changed their company policy on how long their errors and omissions insurance would cover brokers who had left the firm. I am guessing that after the 2008 crisis they saw a rise in claims. For those who may not know, errors and omissions insurance is like malpractice insurance for people in insurance and financial services, and one of the responsibilities of this insurance is to pay for legal expenses of any potential lawsuits. Unfortunately, in my case the insurance was not going to cover the cost of defending me, because I had changed companies, which left me uninsured.

To make a long story short, rather than paying thousands of dollars in legal fees and flying to California for a week for an arbitration hearing, I chose to settle the case in mediation. I had to pay

$4,999, and my previous broker/dealer paid the remaining amount of the $15,000 settlement, as they were also part of the lawsuit. Now I have a permanent black mark on my otherwise-clean record, but some things just can't be helped. I sincerely hope my clients found peace with the outcome.

The reason I share this story with you is not only to come clean but also to make a point. Yes, some annuities can be complex products, and it is a good idea to understand completely before purchasing. But you can say the same thing about everything else, wouldn't you agree? When used appropriately, annuities can provide many benefits.

CHAPTER 10

LONG-TERM CARE AND THE DESI COMMUNITY

My mission in life is not merely to survive, but to thrive; and to do so with some passion, some compassion, some humor, and some style.

—MAYA ANGELOU

From what I've observed in working within the Indian American community for the last twenty-five years, the majority of the community has been lax when it comes to long-term care insurance. Perhaps it is because traditionally, in India, when the parents get older, they often live with their children and depend on the children to take care of them. For many, the expectation is that the same traditions will continue here in the United States.

SURVEY: DO YOU PLAN ON LIVING WITH YOUR CHILDREN IN RETIREMENT?

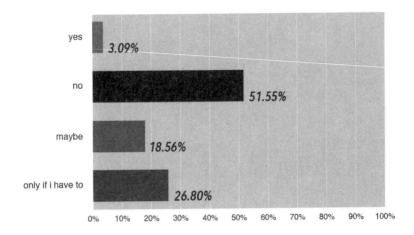

Of course, this is a possibility, and hopefully our children will continue our cultural values. But there are some problems with this thought. Many in newer generations don't share the same cultural values. I know that my parents are always welcome in our home, and we'll be happy to take care of them. We even have a bedroom and bathroom on the main floor specifically for them. But can I expect the same from my kids, who were born and raised in the United States? I am not sure!

Today, we have no idea who our children will marry and what values their future husbands and wives will hold. The other challenge is that in most households in the United States, both spouses work and often travel for their work. Many times, your children may be living on the other side of the country or the world from you, making it difficult to be your caretaker on a daily basis.

Some in the Indian community I have talked to about long-term care believe that if they ever needed care like that, they would just move back to India, where they believe the costs of care would be much cheaper. There are some problems with that plan as well.

Think about it for a minute. You may be in your eighties when you need care and possibly assistance in daily living activities such as bathing, going to the bathroom, and getting in and out of a car—would you really want to move to a country like India, where day-to-day living is hard enough even when you are healthy? Would you really want to leave your family and friends to try to save some money? Probably not!

My point is that you may have worked hard your entire life. You put your children through college, got them married, and took care of your family and your parents, so why not take the extra steps and set up a long-term care plan for you and your spouse so that you can spend your golden years with dignity?

SURVEY: DO YOU HAVE A LONG-TERM CARE PLAN IN PLACE FOR THE HEALTHCARE COSTS IN RETIREMENT

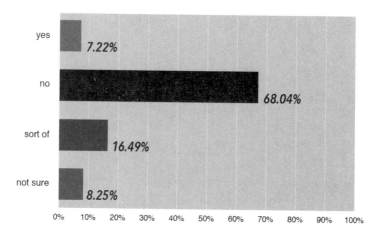

Many people have misconceptions about what long-term care is, how much it costs, and who pays for it. Let me try and make it a little clearer for you. Generally, Medicare and individual health insurance policies pay a very limited amount for long-term care expenses because long-term care is about custodial care, not skilled nursing care.

Why not take the extra steps and set up a long-term care plan for you and your spouse so that you can spend your golden years with dignity?

Custodial care is associated with needing assistance with daily living activities such as eating, bathing, dressing, going to the bathroom, transferring to a wheelchair, and so forth. Medicare and health insurance policies generally pay for more of your skilled nursing care costs but not so much for custodial care.

Long-term care can be provided in several ways. Most often, it is provided as a home healthcare benefit, where someone comes to your home on an ongoing basis to help you with your daily living activities. Other times, it is given in an assisted-living facility where you live and there is a staff of nurses and caretakers who can assist you on a daily basis. When there is a need for constant supervised medical attention, a person may be required to move into a nursing-home facility.

AVERAGE COSTS FOR LONG-TERM CARE SERVICES

If you look at the average costs of long-term care in the United States, it is astonishing. Here are some average costs for various services on a national basis, courtesy of Genworth Life Insurance Company, from the 2015 Cost of Care Survey. Please keep in mind these are average costs around the United States. The costs in your state could be higher or lower based on many variables, including the location, quality, and experience of service providers.

---

homemaker services: $20/hour, $44,616/year

home health aide services: $20/hour $45,760/year

adult day care: $69/day, $17,940/year

assisted living: $3600/month, $43,200/year

nursing home (semiprivate): $220/day, $80,300/year

nursing home (private room): $250/day, $91,250/year[11]

As you can see, it can get pretty expensive—especially with certain conditions such as Alzheimer's that can last for many years, such as in the example of President Ronald Reagan, who was diagnosed with Alzheimer's around 1994 and died in 2004 at age ninety-three.[12]

Many people start out paying these long-term care custodial costs from their savings but eventually spend all of their assets and end up on Medicaid for support. The problem with that is that while they are spending down their assets to qualify for Medicaid, they are also spending down their spouse's assets, leaving them impoverished. Actuarially speaking, women outlive men, so it is women who most often end up being the caretakers and are left without enough assets for their retirement.

---

11   "The Cost of Long-Term Care in the United States," SeniorHomes.com, https://www.seniorhomes.com/p/costs/.

12   "Ronald Raegan," Wikipedia, https://en.wikipedia.org/wiki/Ronald_Reagan.

WHAT IS MEDICAID?

For those of you who are not familiar with it, Medicaid is a joint federal and state government program that helps people with low income and assets pay for some or all of their healthcare bills. It covers medical care, like doctor visits and hospital costs, long-term care services in nursing homes, and long-term care services provided at home. Unlike Medicare, Medicaid does pay for custodial care in nursing homes and at home.

Generally, the rules for who is eligible for Medicaid and what services are covered are based on federal requirements, but each state has considerable leeway in how they operate their programs. To be eligible for Medicaid you must meet certain requirements, including having income and assets that do not exceed the levels used by your state.

Medicaid qualification has become more difficult over the years. In some states, you may have to be a US citizen to qualify, which kind of makes sense. They don't want people to immigrate to this country and get free healthcare.

Keep in mind that being on Medicaid is not always a desirable thing. When you are on Medicaid, you may also be giving up some freedom of choice. You may not get a private room, and you may have to go to a facility where Medicaid beds are available, because most long-term care facilities limit the number of Medicaid beds they allow (their reimbursement rates for those are usually much lower than those of fee-paying clients).

LONG-TERM CARE INSURANCE PLANNING

*Don't tell me where your priorities are. Show me where
you spend your money and I'll tell you what they are.*

—JAMES W. FRICK

As we can see based on the trends of aging and healthcare costs, the threats of long-term care costs in retirement are very real. One of the easiest ways to minimize the risks of the high cost of long-term care services is with some long-term care insurance.

Fortunately, we have many options for long-term care insurance in the marketplace today.

Traditional Long-Term Care Insurance

With traditional long-term care insurance, you choose a daily benefit amount (for example, $200 per day) and a benefit period (for example, five years). You typically have a waiting period before the benefits will begin (for example, ninety days), and you also have options for inflation-protection riders, which allow your long-term care benefits to be increased each year either by a fixed percentage of 3 to 5 percent or tied to the CPI, which is how we measure inflation in this country. This could be very important because if you purchased your policy while you were in your fifties and you don't use your benefits until you are eighty, you want to be able to keep up with the inflation during those thirty years.

Life Insurance and Annuities with Long-Term Care Benefits

We also have life insurance policies that offer optional long-term care riders. By combining cash value life insurance and long-term care benefits, you can provide additional living benefits for yourself as well as death benefits for your loved ones. Some policies allow you to make lump sum contributions so that you do not have to make annual payments for your entire life. This is a popular strategy for some people. The following is an interesting case study on life insurance with long-term care benefits.

Case Study

Mr. and Mrs. Kapur are sixty years old and in very good health. They don't believe they will need long-term care in the future, but to be on the safe side, they are keeping an extra $200,000 in their bank CDs for the purpose of potential long-term care expenses. That money is not earning much interest at this time.

Their advisor showed them an insurance product that allows them to make a lump sum contribution into a life insurance policy with long-term care benefits. By contributing the $200,000 they have set aside for long-term care into the policy, they were able to get $395,000 in long-term care benefits along with the same $395,000 in death benefit.

If the Kapurs need long-term care in the future, they will now have access to much more than the $200,000 they previously had set aside. If they never use the benefits, their beneficiaries will receive the $395,000 as a tax-free life insurance death benefit after the second person's death. Some policies also allow the insured to withdraw their original principal at any time, without any surrender penalties. So if the Kapurs ever decide that they don't want this policy, they can get their original $200,000 back.

Some companies and policies also allow for partial benefits that may be used in other parts of the world, so if you are planning on retiring in India or other parts of the world, you may still be able to use some of your benefits overseas. This is not a bad option for people who have a need for long-term care insurance and are sitting on large amounts of cash earning low interest rates.

We also have some annuity products that provide optional long-term care benefits. These products, like the life insurance policies, offer a dual benefit. They may be used to grow your money tax-deferred, either for retirement income or to be accessed for long-term care benefits.

Some hybrid annuity products give you the ability to multiply your long-term care benefits by offering as much as three times the annuity's values for potential long-term care expenses. The benefits are based on your age and health and can vary from company to company.

These features also make them an attractive choice for people who currently have fixed annuities and would like to transfer their annuities to include these benefits. Consider all of your options before making appropriate decisions.

As we have discussed, long-term care planning is something that can be easily overlooked, especially when we are not accustomed to it culturally. But it is an important subject that needs to be addressed. We hope our children will be able to take care of us in our old age, but for various reasons, they may not be able to. It is up to us to do the appropriate planning so that we may lead the end of our lives with peace and dignity.

CHAPTER 11

HEALTH INSURANCE PLANNING FOR PARENTS MOVING TO THE UNITED STATES FROM ABROAD

Money isn't everything . . . but it ranks right up there with oxygen.

—RITA DAVENPORT

The following is a true story. Last year, I had a client whose father immigrated to the United States from India. Her father was very ill, and they wanted to bring him here and make sure he got adequate attention and healthcare. Of course, the biggest concern was health insurance and the coverage of preexisting conditions. After talking to her for a while, we were able to help her find coverage that they were able to take advantage of. Unfortunately, after nine months in the United States, her father's health deteriorated very rapidly, and he passed away. The healthcare expenses were over $100,000. We were fortunate that we were able to insure him and that he was able to get some excellent healthcare and spend his last days surrounded by his family.

Many in our community have parents who decide to move to the United States from India and other parts of the world to live with their families. This sometimes becomes a challenge because health insurance can be expensive, and the parents often have health issues. The good news is that with the passing of the Affordable Care Act (ACA), also known as "Obamacare," it is now possible for us to insure people over age sixty-five who are not eligible for Medicare or Medicaid.

I have seen the health insurance industry change drastically over the last several decades. In some ways it has gotten better, and in other ways it has gotten much worse. With the passing of the ACA, many of the rules for insurance companies have changed.

Health insurance companies are now required to accept every legal resident with all preexisting health conditions and to offer the minimum essential benefits, including routine preventive physicals, maternity benefits, and unlimited lifetime maximums.

Just a few years ago, if we had a person over age sixty-five who wanted health insurance, we had very few options for them even if they were healthy because most health insurance companies did not offer coverage for them. This was also a problem for people who had other health conditions, like diabetes. But now we are able to insure most people!

The downside is that health insurance premiums have gone through the roof, and we do not know when they will stabilize. We have been seeing insurance premiums that doubled for many people when the ACA was first implemented, and we are also seeing rate increases in double digits each year. There are quite a few people who have benefited from the ACA with tax credits and cost sharing. Here are the three main requirements to qualify for ACA subsidies.

There are quite a few people who have benefited from the ACA with tax credits and cost sharing.

QUALIFYING FOR ACA SUBSIDIES

In 2016, there are three main requirements to qualify for ACA subsidies. Note that these rules may change in the future and may also vary from state to state. Please consult your insurance professional for the rules in your state.

1. **Legal residency:** You must have a valid green card or US citizenship. A visitor visa does not qualify for coverage or any tax credits. Other legal statuses may also be acceptable. For a complete list and more information, go to www. healthcare.gov.

2. **Income requirement:** In most states where Medicaid expansion has not been implemented, there is a minimum-income requirement that a person must have to qualify for tax credits to help pay for health insurance premiums. The income requirements are based on federal poverty level guidelines, which are based on the number of people in your household and the household income. If your income is either below or above the income limits, you will not be eligible for tax credits. Please Google current limits for exact numbers.

3. **You must file taxes:** The other requirement is that the person receiving the tax credits must also file a tax return in the United States and cannot be a dependent on someone else's tax returns. The eligibility is based on your adjusted gross income for that year. The counted income includes most sources, including wages, Social Security, interest earnings, and pensions, as well as excluded nontaxable foreign income. Once again, please consult with your insurance professionals or visit healthcare.gov for more information.

Here is an example of how some people are qualifying for tax credits and subsidies for their elderly parents based on current rules of the ACA.

Case Study 1

Mr. Shah's parents, who are seventy years old, moved to the States recently to live with their children and grandchildren. Although they are in generally good health, the father has diabetes and the mother has high blood pressure. The parents do not currently work in the United States and have zero income.

If Mr. Shah purchases health insurance policies for his parents, the premiums are estimated to be from $1,400 to $2,500 per month based on benefits, networks, and plan types. Mr. Shah also owns a hotel, and his father often helps him out in the business but isn't currently getting paid to do so. Mr. Shah decides to give his father a paycheck of $1,500 a month through the business and will also not claim him as a tax dependent so that they can each file their own taxes.

The result is that the Shah parents now receive around $1,400 a month in tax credits as well as reductions on their deductibles and out-of-pocket costs. They are now able to purchase a health insurance policy from the health insurance marketplace for $125 a month with a deductible of $500 per person and an out-of-pocket maximum of $750 per individual. Their new policy will also provide them with office-visit copays and prescription benefits and will cover all of their preexisting health conditions.

Case Study 2

Mr. Rahman, a widower with two young children, asked his mother to move from India to live with him and help him take care of his children. His mother is sixty-five years old and does not have any income.

Mr. Rahman decided to pay his mother a salary of $1,200 a month to take care of the children. Mrs. Rahman will also file her own taxes. She is now eligible for $695 a month in tax credits and is eligible to purchase a health insurance policy from the marketplace with a premium of $70 a month. Her policy will cover the minimum essential benefits as provided by the ACA.

These are just some of the examples of how people are able to get tax credits and health insurance coverage for their parents when the parents are not eligible for Medicare or Medicaid.

It is important to stress here that these are the current rules in 2017, and as we know, things can change—especially with a new president coming into office with intentions of repealing and replacing Obamacare. We don't know how all this will play out but I can foresee some changes coming our way. It is also important to realize that many insurance companies are becoming a lot stricter and asking for proof of Medicare and Medicaid ineligibility, which means you may have to go through the application process for Medicare or Medicaid and provide rejection letters to show ineligibility.

CHAPTER 12

BASICS OF ESTATE PLANNING

Estate planning is an important and everlasting gift
you can give your family. And setting up a smooth
inheritance isn't as hard as you might think.

—SUZE ORMAN

The Indian American community has done quite well as hoteliers, computer professionals, doctors, and small-business owners. Many have accumulated massive amounts of wealth, but few have done enough (or any) estate planning.

Many have misconceptions about estate planning. Some

Many have misconceptions about estate planning. Some people believe that they only need to do estate planning if they are very wealthy.

people believe that they only need to do estate planning if they are very wealthy. Others believe that all of their assets will automatically go to their spouse and children after their death and that they do not need to do anything. Let me tell you—that is not always true! Everybody needs some form of basic estate planning because estate planning affects not only what happens to our assets upon our death but also what happens to them while we are alive.

SURVEY: HAVE YOU DONE YOUR ESTATE PLANNING? (WILLS, POWER OF ATTORNEY, TRUSTS, ETC.)

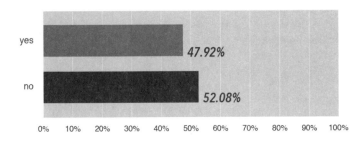

I have broken up estate planning into two chapters. Chapter 12, Basics of Estate Planning, explains the importance of estate planning and the fundamentals we need to consider in our planning. Chapter 13, Planning for Estate Taxes, discusses advanced estate planning, some of the challenges wealthy individuals face, and possible solutions to those challenges.

Let's begin with the four basic elements of estate planning.

1. **Wealth accumulation:** Wealth accumulation is just that. How do we accumulate wealth that we can use during our lifetime and then pass on to our family? What are the most efficient ways of growing our money so that we can get good use of it while we are alive? We have talked

about many wealth-accumulation strategies in some of the previous chapters.

2. **Wealth preservation:** There are many things that threaten our wealth, including divorce, disability, death of a loved one, health issues, bankruptcy, and liabilities from business partners, to name just a few. Wealth preservation is the risk-management component and involves proper insurance planning to preserve wealth, corporate structures to protect against liabilities, and sometimes prenuptial agreements for wealthy individuals planning to marry.

3. **Wealth distribution:** What is the most effective way to transfer our assets to our family with minimum taxes and erosion? This could include life insurance policies, annual gifting within the gifting allowances, family limited partnerships, various forms of trusts, and many other advanced planning strategies.

4. **Asset protection:** In a country with millions of civil lawsuits every year, the chances of being sued in your lifetime are very high. Asset-protection strategies allow us to protect our assets from various liabilities as well as frivolous lawsuits.

I realize that estate planning is an uncomfortable topic for many people. No one wants to think about his or her own death. I have seen many people tear up while discussing their mortality and that of their spouse and loved ones, but this is a very important topic.

We have seen many people procrastinate until it's too late. After their death, their families end up trying to figure out where all the assets are, or they are taken advantage of by their spouse's business partners or employees. Some end up in legal battles that last for years, with a good portion of their wealth lost to unintended third parties, taxes, and legal fees. There are hundreds of stories of famous people who built great fortunes just to have their wealth deteriorate by not doing proper estate planning. There are just as many stories of ordinary people who did not put in place the most basic documents to make their family's lives simpler upon their passing. And it is just sad because it's really not that difficult. You just need to get it started and get it done.

I would encourage you to look at estate planning as an opportunity to take an active role in what happens to your assets after your passing and to ease your family into managing without you. We often ask clients to think about the first morning after your death, as morbid as that might be, because it highlights the main issues at stake. Where would your family go to find your financial documents? Would they be able to access the bank accounts? Would they know anything about running your business? These are very basic, everyday issues and have nothing to do with how much money you have.

Case Study

Mr. Vaswani, a forty-five-year-old business owner dies unexpectedly, leaving behind a wife and two teenage children. Mrs. Vaswani has well-meaning relatives and friends trying to help her, but essentially she has to make a number of big decisions, such as whether she should keep the business or sell it. If she doesn't sell it quickly, then she risks the value going down. To complicate the matter, the husband had not written a will, so on top of everything else she has to do, a probate petition needs to be filed, requesting that the court appoint her as the representative for her husband's estate. That process can take anywhere from six to eight weeks in the easy states and up to four to six *months* in other states. Additionally, because there are minor children, the court will most likely appoint a guardian to protect the children. You may be wondering why the courts would appoint a guardian when the mother is still living. This can vary based on state laws, but in some states, the court systems appoint a guardian to determine if the mother has the qualifications to manage the assets of the children. This is separate from physical custody, which is not at issue. This increases the cost and time of the probate. Finally, because there is no will and there are both a surviving spouse and children, Mr. and Mrs. Vaswani's assets will be divided in accordance with state law, which means Mrs. Vaswani may not get all the assets and may have to share with her children. Most of this could have been avoided with a simple will, or even better, a living trust, which would allow Mrs. Vaswani to step into her husband's shoes upon his death.

There have been many cases of family members who have received large sums of inheritances and have squandered them within a very short time. I believe this is because many times, the people receiving the inheritances do not know how to handle the funds—similar to lottery winners who find themselves broke after a short time. You can use estate planning as an opportunity to initiate the conversation, educate your family on proper wealth-management techniques, and share with them your intentions on what and how they should spend your hard-earned money.

Good estate planning can help eliminate confusion among family members. Let's say you have three daughters and some family jewelry. As a part of your plan, you can dictate which daughter gets what. You may even choose to gift to them while you are living.

If you feel you have a spendthrift son or daughter and you want to give them access to money on a gradual or controlled basis, you can give specific instructions to your executors and trustees so that your wishes can be carried out.

If you have a special-needs child who you know will need support for his or her entire life, you can establish a special-needs trust for that child, with individual or corporate trustees (such as a bank or a trust company) so that your child can get lifelong support.

If you want a special gift to go to your grandkids every year for Diwali or Christmas after your passing, we can show you how to make that happen. Sometimes, this can even be accomplished with a life insurance policy. You also have an opportunity to make a charitable impact. Charitable giving in estate planning can help reduce estate taxes, capital gains taxes, and income taxes while allowing you to support your favorite charitable causes. The point is that this is your opportunity to use your wealth in a way that best suits you and your family.

Estate planning is also about taking care of yourself while you are living. In the event of an accident or illness that renders you unable to make decisions for yourself, who would you want to nominate to make healthcare and financial decisions for you? Many times, they can only do that if you have the proper documents in place. Proper estate planning puts those documents in place *before* disaster strikes.

Estate planning is even more important for immigrants, who may have assets in multiple countries because different rules may be applicable for each country. You will need to do some estate planning in each country where you have assets. Additionally, if you have not been disclosing foreign assets during your lifetime, you will be leaving a huge problem for your spouse and children to clean up with the IRS. Believe me, leaving a tax issue for your family to deal with is not recommended.

Although you can try and do it yourself, I recommend that you use qualified attorneys to help you create the documents for you. This is not something you do often, so why not spend a little time and money and get it done right? A good attorney or financial planner may also ask important questions to prompt some additional thinking and may also offer additional solutions that you haven't thought about. I would recommend that you use an attorney who specializes in estate planning, especially if you have a complicated situation.

BASIC ESTATE PLANNING

When planning for posterity, we ought to
remember virtue is not hereditary.

—THOMAS PAINE

For most people, there are three basic estate-planning documents worth having.

1. Last will and testament: Your will allows you to spell out specifically who, what, and when someone gets your assets after your death. For example, if you have minor children, you may not want them to have access to all of your wealth until they are mature enough. So you can specify in your will that they should have some money coming to them at age eighteen when they are ready for college and the remainder at different intervals as they get older. If you have jewelry that you want to leave to a specific son or daughter, you can spell that out in your will. If you want to make specific bequests to other family members, you can specify that in your will.

2. Durable powers of attorney for healthcare and finance: This goes back to what I said earlier. What if you were involved in a car accident and were incapacitated for an extended period of time? Who would you want to make your healthcare and financial decisions for you?

Depending on where you live, the person you choose to make decisions may be called one of the following:

- healthcare agent

- healthcare proxy

- healthcare surrogate

- healthcare representative

- healthcare attorney-in-fact

- patient advocate[13]

You can appoint a separate person for healthcare and financial tasks, if you wish. For example, if you feel your spouse would be too attached to make healthcare decisions for you, you may want to appoint another family member. The same applies to your financial affairs. You can appoint whomever you feel will do a better job when it comes to your finances. Sometimes it may be a business partner or a friend.

Case Study

Mr. Rahman is a small-business owner, and he is the only person listed on his business checking accounts. His durable powers of attorney for healthcare and finances were established; he nominated his wife to make the healthcare decisions on his behalf and his son to make the financial decisions.

---

13 "Living wills and advance directives for medical decisions," Mayo Clinic, November 11, 2014, http://www.mayoclinic.org/healthy-lifestyle/consumer-health/in-depth/living-wills/art-20046303.

Last year Mr. Rahman had a stroke, and he was not able to take care of his business for an extended period of time. His wife was able to make healthcare decisions on his behalf, and his son was able to make the financial decisions to keep his business running until he recovered.

You also have the option to appoint multiple people for each task, but that may not be a good idea, as it makes it much more difficult to get things done when two or more parties have to agree on, and in some cases, sign off on, everything. Appointing successor persons, on the other hand, is a great idea, in case the person you had appointed is not able or willing to do the job. In that situation, the successor you appointed is able to make financial and healthcare decisions on your behalf. Just remember, all of this is flexible while you are in good health. If you ever want to change your appointees, you just need to draft up revised documents.

3. Living will: A living will is not the same thing as the last will and testament. A living will is basically your advanced directive to the family if you are ever on a life-support system and the doctor says that the chance of recovery is very small. Your advance directive shares your wishes on whether your family should keep you alive on life support or remove you from the life-support system. As you can imagine, this is a very difficult decision for families to make.

You should address a number of possible end-of-life care decisions in your living will:

- **Resuscitation** restarts the heart when it has stopped beating. Determine if and when you would want to be resuscitated by cardiopulmonary resuscitation (CPR) or by a device that delivers an electric shock to stimulate the heart.

- **Mechanical ventilation** takes over your breathing if you're unable to do so. Consider if, when, and for how long you would want to be placed on a mechanical ventilator.

- **Tube feeding** supplies the body with nutrients and fluids intravenously or via a tube in the stomach. Decide if, when, and for how long you would want to be fed in this manner.

- **Dialysis** removes waste from your blood and manages fluid levels if your kidneys no longer function. Determine if, when, and for how long you would want to receive this treatment.

- **Antibiotics or antiviral** medications can be used to treat many infections. If you were near the end of life, would you want infections to be treated aggressively or would you rather let infections run their course?

- **Comfort care (palliative care)** includes any number of interventions that may be used to keep you comfortable and manage pain, while abiding by your other treatment wishes. This may include being allowed to die at home, getting pain medications, being fed ice chips to soothe dryness, and avoiding invasive tests or treatments.

- **Organ and tissue donations** for transplantation can be specified in your living will. If your organs are removed for donation, you will be kept on life-sustaining treatment temporarily until the procedure is complete.

To help your agent avoid any confusion, you may want to state in your living will that you understand the need for this temporary intervention.

- **Donating your body** for scientific study also can be specified. Contact a local medical school, university, or donation program for information on how to register for a planned donation for research.[14]

Your directive makes things much easier. This is also why, when you go into a hospital for a surgery or major procedure, the hospital will sometimes make you fill out a living-will document—just in case.

FOUR WAYS TO TRANSFER PROPERTY

When someone passes away, there are four basic ways we transfer assets from one person to another (in the United States). Basically, transferring assets boils down to two main categories: probate and nonprobate.

1. **By contract or beneficiary designations:** Your life insurance policies, IRAs, 401(k)s, and annuities all have beneficiary designations. All of these bypass your will and go directly to the named beneficiaries upon your death, making them a very efficient way to transfer your wealth. Unlike a will, a beneficiary designation cannot be contested. Whoever you chose on your policy will get your account. This is why you want to make sure your beneficiary designations are

---

14   "Living wills and advance directives for medical decisions," Mayo Clinic, November 11, 2014, http://www.mayoclinic.org/healthy-lifestyle/consumer-health/in-depth/living-wills/art-20046303.

updated based on your current wishes. If you got divorced and your ex-spouse is still the beneficiary of your life insurance policy, your current spouse is not going to be very happy with the outcome! The life insurance company has to give the death benefit to the person who is on the contract.

2. Joint tenants with rights of survivorship: For married couples, joint tenancy with rights of survivorship is the most common way to own property like your home or bank accounts. In the event of a death, the joint tenant automatically has the rights to those assets. But after the death of the second spouse, it has to go through a legal process called *probate* to transfer the asset to the person(s) specified in your will.

Joint tenants with rights of survivorship should not be confused with *joint tenants in common*, where each person on the account owns his or her own portion equally. We often see joint tenants in common accounts in business and partnership accounts. They were also very common in same-sex couples before the legalization of gay marriage. Often, banks and other financial-service companies offer an option to the account holders where upon death, the account can be transferred to the named beneficiaries. If transfer on death hasn't been established on a tenants in common account, it would have to go through probate.

3. Probate: This is the legal process that takes place after someone dies. This is done typically by your executor of the will, who has to file papers in probate court to prove the validity of your will in order to distribute your assets. If there is no will, then the judge may appoint a person who will be in charge of administering your estate.

Most of the time it is a family member or someone who will be receiving the bulk of your estate.

The executor of your will or the person in charge of administering your estate will be responsible for identifying your assets, finding family members who are the intended beneficiaries, paying off any debts you may have, and distributing your assets to your intended beneficiaries after paying off any creditors. This process can be time consuming depending upon the size of your estate, the location of your property, and the legal processes involved in those states or countries.

Your executor may also have to decide if any assets have to be sold in order to provide cash liquidity that may be required to pay off any debts, make any cash bequests that you requested in your will, or pay off any estate taxes that may be due.

As you can tell, this can be an involved process and requires some thought on your part on whom you should name as your executor. Many times in our community, the executor named may be in India, making it difficult for them to administer the estate. It is also not a bad idea to get assistance from qualified attorneys to help you through this process, especially if you are not sure what and how it needs to be done.

The three biggest challenges of probate are loss of privacy, delays due to the legal process, and potential legal expenses if you hire an attorney to help you. If you own assets in multiple states, your estate might have to go through probate in those states as well.

Whenever someone dies with an estate that has to go through probate, the courts require that the death be publicized in the newspapers so that if there are outstanding debts, the creditors have the opportunity to claim on the estate. The delays of probate can last up to nine months, which can be challenging for family members who might need access to the funds during that time.

According to AARP, probate can cost up to 10 percent of your gross estate before debts are paid, depending on the type of assets you own and the legal fees of your attorney(s). Of course, if all you have is your home, and your family can do the probate work themselves, the cost of probating can be pretty reasonable.

Keep in mind that a will can be contested much more easily than a living trust. If a family member or a business partner feels that you accidentally left them out of the will and/or you had indicated that you were going to leave a particular asset to them, they may contest your will, and that can add to the probate delays and expenses for your family. There are plenty of stories of contested wills of the rich and famous, including Howard Hughes, Anna Nicole Smith, and many others.

So how do we avoid probate and some of the challenges that come with it? This is where a revocable living trust comes in as an estate-planning tool.

4. Revocable living trusts: As its name states, this trust is revocable, meaning that you can change the terms of the document at any time, just like your will. It uses your Social Security number, and you are the trustee of your trust while you are alive, so it is treated the same as your own assets. A revocable living trust is also sometimes referred to as a *credit shelter trust*, which is a trust that lets you utilize your unified estate and gift tax credits for estate tax planning, which we will discuss in the next chapter.

Let's go back to the example of Mr. Rahman, who had a stroke and had established durable powers of attorney so that his family could make healthcare and financial decisions on his behalf. If he had established a revocable living trust and appointed his wife and son as trustees, they would have been able to step into his shoes automatically as trustees and would have been able to handle his affairs while he was recovering. A revocable living trust can be a good alternative to the durable power of attorneys. Assets that are held in a revocable living trust can also avoid the costs and delays associated with probate and may also help maintain your family's privacy.

What assets can be placed in a living trust? Generally speaking, your retirement accounts, life insurance policies, and annuities cannot be (and do not need to be) placed inside your living trust, as they transfer with beneficiary designations. The most common things that are placed in living trusts are homes and other real estate, bank accounts, and brokerage accounts. Many times people also leave their trusts as the recipient of their insurance policies so that the trustee can distribute the funds based on trust instructions.

Who should consider a living trust? It depends on the type of assets you have. If all you have are life insurance policies, retirement accounts that will pass to heirs with beneficiary designations, and a home that you believe your family can probate, you may not need a living trust.

If, on the other hand, you have real estate in multiple states and multiple brokerage and bank accounts, a living trust may be a good investment for you. The cost of a living trust package is not significantly more than that of a will package. Check with your attorney for pricing.

As you can tell, the basic estate-planning documents should be done by most people. Even if you don't have many assets, the powers of attorney and living will can help your family make important decisions on your behalf, and you can also choose which family member you trust to make those decisions.

CHAPTER 13

PLANNING FOR ESTATE TAXES

*You must pay taxes. But there's no law
that says you gotta leave a tip.*

—MORGAN STANLEY ADVERTISEMENT

In the previous chapter, we discussed some of the challenges of wealth preservation, including divorces, lawsuits, and spendthrift beneficiaries. But let's not forget estate taxes. For people whose net worth exceeds the current individual estate tax limits (which, as of 2017, are currently at $5,490,000 for an individual or $10,980,000 for a married couple), you may have an estate tax problem.[15] Your net worth is calculated by taking all of your assets, including your

---

15   "Estate Taxation," ElderLawAnswers, March 3, 2016, http://www.elderlawanswers.com/estate-taxation-12091.

home, retirement accounts, and business interests, and subtracting the liabilities, such as mortgages and other loan obligations.

Estate tax planning can be complicated, as there are many rules, and I will tell you in advance that if you believe you have an estate tax problem, you should get expert advice. Many people in our community have haphazardly transferred hotels, real estate, and other assets to their children and found themselves with additional gift tax problems. This is just a brief overview to help you start thinking. Let's start with some of the basics.

What is included in your estate? Generally speaking, everything you own is included in your estate, including your home, retirement accounts, annuities, businesses, stocks, bonds, partnership shares, your share of joint accounts, and life insurance policies. When I say life insurance policies, I mean the actual face amount of the policy, not just the cash value (a common misconception with cash value policies). If you have a $5 million life insurance policy and you are the owner of the policy, guess what? That is a part of your estate and may be subject to estate tax liability. Even your assets in India and around the world are included as part of your estate.

When are estate taxes due? If both spouses are US citizens, estate taxes are not due upon the death of the first spouse. The entire estate can be transferred to the surviving spouse with the unlimited marital deduction. This means that Bill Gates can transfer all of his billions to his wife, Melinda, upon his death (and vice versa) without any estate taxes. But at the death of the second spouse, the estate taxes would be due.

For non-US citizens and nonresident aliens, the rules are a little different and can be complex because they depend upon the residence and citizen status of each spouse. Please refer to the following chart for reference.

NON-CITIZEN RESIDENT ESTATE/GIFT TAX QUICK REFERENCE GUIDE 2016

	CITIZEN MARRIED TO RESIDENT OR NON-RESIDENT ALIEN	RESIDENT ALIEN MARRIED TO RESIDENT OR NON-RESIDENT ALIEN	RESIDENT ALIEN MARRIED TO CITIZEN	NON-RESIDENT ALIEN MARRIED TO CITIZEN	NON-RESIDENT ALIEN MARRIED TO RESIDENT ALIEN	NON-RESIDENT ALIEN MARRIED TO NON-RESIDENT ALIEN
MARITAL DEDUCTION	No marital deduction (QDOT exception)	No marital deduction (QDOT exception)	Unlimited marital deduction	Unlimited marital deduction	No marital deduction (QDOT exception)	No marital deduction (QDOT exception)
EXEMPTION EQUIVALENT FOR ESTATE TAXES	$5,450,000 exemption equivalent in 2016	$5,450,000 exemption equivalent in 2016	$5,450,000 exemption equivalent in 2016	$60,000 exemption equivalent in 2016	$60,000 exemption equivalent in 2016	$60,000 exemption equivalent in 2016
EXEMPTION EQUIVALENT FOR GIFT TAXES	$5,450,000 exemption equivalent in 2016	$5,450,000 exemption equivalent in 2016	$5,450,000 exemption equivalent in 2016	Not available	Not available	Not available
WORLDWIDE TAXATION OF PROPERTY	Property taxed worldwide	Property taxed worldwide	Property taxed worldwide	Property taxed in the U.S. only	Property taxed in the U.S. only	Property taxed in the U.S. only
ANNUAL EXCLUSION GIFT TO ALIEN SPOUSE	Annual exclusion gift of $148,000 in 2016	Annual exclusion gift of $148,000 in 2016	Not applicable	Not applicable	Annual exclusion gift of $148,000 in 2016	Annual exclusion gift of $148,000 in 2016
ANNUAL EXCLUSION GIFT TO OTHERS	Annual exclusion gift of $14,000 in 2016	Annual exclusion gift of $14,000 in 2016	Annual exclusion gift of $14,000 in 2016	Annual exclusion gift of $14,000 in 2016	Annual exclusion gift of $14,000 in 2016	Annual exclusion gift of $14,000 in 2016

There are two basic ways for spouses who are not US citizens to address the issue of limited marital gifting.

1. **Become a US citizen.** If your noncitizen spouse becomes a US citizen by the time estate taxes are due, which is about nine months after death (you may also be eligible for a six-month extension from the IRS), this will allow your spouse to claim the unlimited marital deduction. Just keep in mind that citizenship proceedings can take time—better to plan for this in advance.

2. **Establish a qualified domestic trust (QDOT).** Your noncitizen spouse can inherit from you free of estate tax if you use a special trust called a *QDOT* (Internal Revenue Code section 2056A). You leave property to the trust instead of directly to your spouse. Your spouse is the beneficiary of the trust; there can't be any other beneficiaries while your spouse is alive. Your spouse receives income that the trust property generates; these amounts are not subject to estate tax.

   If trust assets themselves (the principal) are distributed to your spouse, however, the estate tax will probably have to be paid on that property. (There's an exception when distributions are made because the spouse has an urgent, immediate need and no other resources.)

   A QDOT must be established, and the property must be transferred to it by the time the estate tax return of the deceased spouse is due. Usually, QDOTs are set up while both spouses are alive and come into existence when one spouse dies. The trustee—that is, the person or entity in charge of trust assets—must be a US citizen or corporation such as a bank or trust company.

How are estate taxes paid? Estate taxes are due about nine months after the death of the person who has the estate tax liability. This sometimes can be an issue for people who do not have liquidity in their estates. If your estate is tied up in multiple hotels, your family may have a decision to make on which property or properties to sell to pay the estate taxes. Many people have found themselves selling their properties for much less than the fair-market values to meet the tax-payment deadlines.

IRREVOCABLE LIFE INSURANCE TRUSTS (ILITS) AND THE USE OF SURVIVORSHIP LIFE INSURANCE POLICIES

Survivorship life insurance policies are one of the most efficient ways to provide estate tax liquidity. A survivorship life insurance policy is a life insurance policy that covers both spouses and pays a death benefit upon the death of the second spouse. Most commonly, this strategy utilizes a combination of an ILIT, the annual gifting exclusion. The current annual gifting allowance for 2017 is $14,000 per year, per person and the estate and gift tax exclusion is $5.49 million. This is used to fund the life insurance policy.

Most often, this is done by a husband and wife gifting certain amounts of money into an ILIT to benefit a child, grandchild, or other family member. These gifts are then utilized by the trustee to pay for the life insurance premiums. This strategy allows the parents not only to reduce the size of their estate each year (via the annual gifts) but also to leverage their gifts with the life insurance policies, which can later be used to pay for estate tax liabilities (if there are any).

In larger estates, where the annual gifting allowance is not enough, some people may use the lifetime gifting allowance along with other advanced planning techniques.

It is important that you follow the rules associated with gifting while utilizing this strategy. One of the requirements is that you inform the people who are receiving the gifts and give them the right to use the money at the time of the gift. This is accomplished by the trustee sending what are known as "Crummey letters," named after *Crummey et al v. Commissioner of Internal Revenue* in 1968, to the people receiving the gifts and letting them know they have up to thirty days to claim them.[16] After that point, the trustee is free to pay for the life insurance premiums. It's a good idea to let your children know the purpose of the gifts so they are not tempted to use them right away.

The use of life insurance policies along with the annual and lifetime gifting allowances is one of the most efficient wealth-transfer strategies available to us because when done correctly, it can avoid gift taxes, the probate process, and the need to liquidate in order to pay for the estate taxes. The other cool advantage is that the death benefit of life insurance is not only federal income tax-free but may also be estate tax-free.

This was just a brief overview of how to provide for estate taxes with life insurance. There are many other strategies that are worth your consideration and don't involve life insurance. It is highly recommended that you work with qualified advisors in these situations. I have often seen people buying these types of life insurance policies in their personal names and actually *adding* liabilities to their current estate tax problems.

---

16 "Crummey trust," Wikipedia, https://en.wikipedia.org/wiki/Crummey_trust.

CHAPTER 14

ADVANCED ESTATE PLANNING

*You don't **pay** taxes—they **take** taxes.*

—CHRIS ROCK

If you have been blessed and have accumulated a significant amount of wealth in this country, you are lucky—not only because you are wealthy but also because you have so many options for growing and preserving your wealth for future generations and to do some significant good with your money. This is a good time to ask what you want your money to do after your passing.

The tax laws in this country favor the rich in so many ways. We have tools available to reduce or eliminate capital gains taxes, income taxes, estate taxes, and gift taxes. You just need to find advisors who know how to use the advanced tools to help you accomplish your goals. Over the years, I have had the opportunity to work with many wealthy individuals, and it has been really fascinating getting to understand their mind-set.

Some believe that wealth should not be passed on to future generations and that it is up to their kids to build their own wealth. Others would like to leave a legacy to be remembered by. There are also some who would like to give their children everything they could ever want, but they don't want to deprive them of the joy of bringing home a paycheck.

What are your thoughts? Would you like to set up a dynasty trust fund for your future generations, like the Rockefellers and Kennedys? Would you like to leave your wealth to some charities? Or would you like to do a combination of several things? Whatever your answer, I just want you to know that you have options. Here are some of the tools of advanced estate planning that may be worth considering, depending on the size of your estate and your estate-planning goals.

Revocable living trusts and credit shelter trusts are the most common advanced planning techniques used to avoid the delays and expenses of probate court, maintain family privacy, and reduce or eliminate estate taxes.

Irrevocable insurance trusts are designed to keep your life insurance policies out of your estate to reduce or eliminate estate taxes.

Charitable trusts and donor-advised funds are designed to help you accomplish your philanthropic goals and at the same time reduce or eliminate your capital gains taxes, income taxes, and estate taxes.

Family limited partnerships / limited liability companies are designed to provide additional asset protection and maintain control of your assets while gifting the shares to your children to reduce potential estate taxes.

Special-needs trusts are designed to take care of children and family members with special needs.

Irrevocable children's trusts are designed to hold and distribute assets to children over time, based on your specific instructions.

These are just some of the tools available to you. There are many more—such as offshore trusts, dynasty trusts, and family trusts—that are designed for your wealth-preservation needs. You really have a lot of resources available, and you owe it to yourself to explore some of these options if you are wealthy.

Why would you want to have your hard-earned money eroded by taxes and other predators when you can take control and be instrumental in what happens to your wealth? You might even consider making a difference in the lives of others.

DO YOU NEED ASSET PROTECTION?

An incompetent lawyer can delay a trial for months or years. A competent lawyer can delay one even longer.

—EVELLE YOUNGER, FORMER
CALIFORNIA DISTRICT ATTORNEY

Many years ago, when I was taking the class for my certification as a Certified Estate Planner, I learned the importance of asset protection, especially for wealthy individuals. It is estimated that there are over 1.2 million lawyers in the United States in all areas of law, including corporate, immigration, civil, litigation, and many other specialized fields.[17] At the time—I was taking the course around 1998—the teacher estimated there were around eight hundred thousand attorneys and forty million civil lawsuits per year in the United States, making the probability of being sued once in your lifetime pretty high.

Ever watch daytime television? Ever notice how many lawyer commercials play all the time? "Have you been hurt in an accident? We can help you collect thousands." "One call, that's all" is a slogan for a very popular law firm. If you are driving down to Florida, you will see large advertising billboards: "Have you lost money in the stock market? Maybe your financial advisor is to blame, and we can help you collect."

Sadly, this is the case in the healthcare industry as well, which makes physicians and healthcare providers overly cautious. As a result, they may put patients through multiple tests before they confirm any diagnosis, which in turn drives up the cost of healthcare.

In other parts of the world, such as England and France, if you sue someone and lose, you are required to pay the other party's legal expenses—this helps prevent frivolous lawsuits. But unfortunately this is not the case in the United States. In the United States, you can sue anyone for just about anything, and when someone sues you, like it or not, you have to defend yourself in a court of law, which costs money. And even if you win, you still have to pay your legal expenses.

What I have learned over the years is that it is important to have some degree of asset protection. I once met a guy who was in a plumbing business, and he said to me, "RJ, I've been sued five times in my lifetime, and I have won every single time. I just can't afford to win anymore lawsuits." I have also been a part of several legal battles

---

17   Ken Laino, "Too Many Lawyers?" Asset Protection Law Journal, July 7, 2011, http://www.assetprotectionlawjournal.com/2011/07/too-many-lawyers/.

in my life, and I can tell you from experience that it's expensive and not much fun!

In chapter 9, I told you about the lawsuit I had with my client over an annuity misunderstanding, but another memorable case occurred back when I used to publish *Khabar* magazine. We had a religious scammer in our community whose name was Anamalai Anamalai. He went by the name Dr. Commander Selvam. The Fox 5 News team in Atlanta did a report on how this guy was using his temple as a way to charge people fees for religious services such as pujas, mantra chanting, and other miscellaneous services. Once he had your credit card, he would overcharge thousands of dollars on it, and when you pointed that out to him and asked for a refund, he would say that in our culture, it is not customary to ask for a refund for religious activities.

We had published a one-page general article on how one needs to be careful with guys like him, which must have affected his business. So he filed a petition for a criminal case against us in India. Yes, India! Just to make our lives more difficult. He also published a tabloid type of paper here in the United States, and he put photos of all of us, including our employees, with criminal case numbers. In a way it was funny, but it wasn't a joke.

To stop him, we had to sue him for defamation, and he counter-sued us for the same. You can imagine how exciting this must have been for the lawyers. He was suing everyone for all kinds of frivolous things, including the board of trustees for a well-respected temple in town, Fox 5 News, Google, and many individuals who had stood up to him for his fraudulent practices. Many of these individuals had four or five different suits with him simultaneously. He was also notorious for not paying his lawyers.

To make a long story short, this ended up costing us over $15,000 in legal fees for a bunch of nothing. We had a stalemate. One of the trustees at the local temple had connections in India, and the petition there was squashed. Dr. Commander Selvam was eventually indicted for thirty-four felony counts and sentenced to twenty-seven years in prison and is currently serving his time. But he did a lot of damage prior to that.

LAWSUITS ARE EXPENSIVE!

I was never ruined but twice—once when I
lost a lawsuit, once when I won one.

—VOLTAIRE

People often fight for principles, and in the litigation world that costs money, especially if there are attorneys involved. This holds true in lawsuits, divorces, partnership disputes, and any other legal disputes.

Whenever there are legal issues, the attorneys usually do not want to resolve it quickly, because it is generally in their best interest to keep things going so they can bill you for their time. Combining this with the legal system in general, which is slow and frustrating, even a simple dispute can take months or years to resolve while your legal expenses continue to add up.

So when it comes to legal disputes, use your head and don't let your ego get the best of you. It is also recommended that you take the time to understand what type of assets are easier to protect in a lawsuit and which ones are harder to protect. A lot of these rules can vary from state to state, but if asset protection is important to you, you should take time to educate yourself and meet with qualified attorneys and financial planners to discuss your options.

The general rule of asset protection is that whatever is in your name could be taken away from you. Imagine for a moment that you are in the process of getting sued. The other party will look for attorneys who are willing to take on his or her case. The attorney will do a basic background check on you to see what assets are available in your name and will determine whether or not it will be easy enough for him to collect.

If the lawyer discovers that there is some low-hanging fruit and that the probability of winning and collecting is great, he will take the case. But what if he discovered that you really do not have many assets that could be collected? Would that lawyer want to take the case? Probably not. And that is your primary objective—you do not want to be attractive to a potential lawsuit.

Keep in mind that your children are subject to the same potential threats as you are, and that by utilizing proven asset-protection techniques, you can preserve your wealth for generations to come.

I do not want to be a fearmonger, but financial threats also come in the form of divorces, spendthrift beneficiaries, lawsuits from business partners and family members, and so on. If you believe your family may be subject to any of these threats, get educated on your options.

Financial planners like myself, along with estate-planning attorneys, help you protect your assets by utilizing certain insurance and financial-planning instruments such as umbrella policies (which increase your liability coverage), annuities, life insurance policies (which are more protected in certain states), and retirement and pension accounts (which are also a little more protected).

You also have the ability to use the legal structures of trusts, limited liability companies, and other corporate structures to help shield you from potential threats.

ADDITIONAL ESTATE-PLANNING TIPS

Now that you have your estate-planning documents and a successor plan in place (as discussed in chapter 12), there are a few more things you should do:

1. **Safe-deposit box:** If you have a safe-deposit box, let your family know where it is and how to get the key. Many times, people leave important items such as cash and jewelry in safe-deposit boxes as well as in the home, and heirs never find out about the assets in the safe-deposit box. This is even more important if you have a safe-deposit box in India, as it may be very difficult to access that.

Case Study

Mr. Amin had done some great estate planning. He had all of his wills and other legal documents prepared by a qualified attorney and also told his family that he kept all of these documents in a safe-deposit box at the local bank. One thing he forgot to do was authorize his executor to open his safe-deposit box. Upon his death, even though his executor knew where the will was, he couldn't access it without getting the courts to nominate him as the executor, and that couldn't be done, because the documents were in the safe-deposit box that he couldn't access. Eventually, it was all resolved, but you can imagine the challenges it must have created for his family. If you are going to use a safe-deposit box, please be sure to authorize your executor or other family members for access.

2. **Letter to spouse:** Leave a letter to a spouse or family that lists all of your assets, including bank-account numbers and brokerage-account numbers and the usernames and

passwords for these accounts. You can also create a small video if you want to leave a final message that the family can view after your passing.

3. **Digital accounts access:** Many people nowadays have online libraries of music, videos, and books that they can access on demand. For example, I have over a thousand audio books in my audible library, as well as a lot of music in my iTunes library. I would like for my kids and grandkids to have access to all those. Leave your account usernames and passwords for your online libraries.

4. **Social media logins:** If you have Facebook, Twitter, LinkedIn, or other social media profiles, you may want to leave those usernames and passwords for your family to inform your friends and colleagues of your passing. Each social media company has different rules on how they handle accounts for deceased individuals. Some social media companies allow your profile to remain active as a deceased person, which can be accessed in the future by your heirs to learn more about your life.

5. **Talk to your family:** Have a heart-to-heart talk with your spouse, children, and other family members about what you would like to happen after your death. Let them know your wishes and intentions. If you have specific philanthropic desires, let them know so they can help you accomplish those.

6. **Give now!:** Don't wait until your death to give all of your wealth to your children and grandchildren. Give some now so that you can see how they spend it and see the joy on their faces.

I know this is a lot to take in and can be depressing. However, estate planning is a very important part of your overall financial planning and it should not be procrastinated. You should try to get this done as soon as possible, if you haven't done it already.

CHAPTER 15

LEAVING A CHARITABLE LEGACY

We make a living by what we get, but we
make a life by what we give.

—WINSTON CHURCHILL

Can I start you out with a joke on charitable giving? An Indian, an American, and a European were having tea one day, and the subject of charitable giving came up. Each was discussing how he decides how much to donate each month. The American said, "At the end of the month, I take all of the money I earn, put it in a basket, and draw a line on the floor. Then I throw the money in the air, and whatever falls on the left side of the line I donate, and whatever falls on the right side I keep." The European said, "That is very interesting! I also put my money in a basket, but I draw a circle on the ground. I throw the money in the air, and whatever falls inside the circle is mine, and whatever is outside I donate." The Indian said, "You guys are crazy with all of your drawing on the floor. My system is much easier! I put my money in a basket each month and throw it up in the air, and whatever stays up is God's!"

Over the years I have done several seminars and articles on charitable giving. It has been my observation that not many people are charitably inclined. I believe that in many cases, it is not that they are uncharitable—it is just that they have lost faith in many of the charities because most of the money they collect goes to administrative expenses and the huge salaries of their CEOs. This disaffection is understandable! I just want to say that there are some good causes out there that are legitimate, and you also have opportunities to give personally to the people you feel are in need and deserving. Don't let a few bad apples change your opinion of charitable giving.

A LESSON FROM WARREN BUFFETT

I was once listening to a Charlie Rose interview with Warren Buffett and Bill and Melinda Gates. Rose asked Buffett why he chose to donate the majority of his wealth to the Gates Foundation. His answer was very interesting.

Buffet said people have invested with him over the years because they believed he could do a better job of investing than they could. But Buffet believed Bill and Melinda could do a better job of distributing *his* wealth than he would.

I thought the honesty and humility of his statement was just awesome. If you go to www.givingpledge.org, you will find a list of some of the wealthiest people in the world who have pledged to donate at least half of their wealth to philanthropy and charitable giving.

What Buffett says to potential pledge members is that after some point, money does not have much utility to you. But it can have significant benefits in the lives of the less fortunate, and you have the power to make that happen. It's something to keep in mind while you are doing your estate planning!

BENEFITS OF CHARITABLE GIVING

When a fellow says it ain't the money but the
principle of the thing, it's the money.

—ARTEMUS WARD

Many of us have done quite well in this great country, and I am sure many of you have been giving back during your lifetimes to those who are not as fortunate as you. You might also be thinking of doing some philanthropic work in a bigger way in your retirement. The good news is that there are a lot of charitable-giving tools you can use in this country not only to get additional tax benefits but also to maximize the effect of your charitable-giving efforts. One of my personal goals is to bring $100 million to worthwhile causes during my lifetime. This is what we call a BHAG—a big hairy audacious goal! I'm not sure if it will happen, but I'll keep the intention and we'll see. If I can accomplish even 1 percent of that, I'll be satisfied.

Since I don't have $100 million I can donate, I will have to undertake my goal with help from charitably inclined people. I love working with people who are charitably inclined. I have found that charitably inclined people are just fun to be around. They are light in their being, compassionate, grateful, and motivated.

This is not to say that they are pushovers and that they just throw money at the problems of the world. The charitably inclined people I know are able to look at world problems with the big picture in mind and work toward making a difference in their own way, one kind act at a time.

For those of you who are working toward a similar goal, I want to share some of the following tools of charitable giving that might be useful in your giving efforts. Of course, you are also welcome to contact me about this, as well as about anything else in this book, through our website at www.RajeshJyotishi.com or my personal e-mail at RJ@ShalinFinancial.com.

Donor-Advised Funds (DAFs)

DAFs have been around since 1931. They started becoming very popular in the 1990s and have been philanthropy's fastest-growing charitable-giving vehicles.[18] DAFs work like this:

- You make an irrevocable contribution of personal assets, which could include cash, stocks, bonds, or real estate.

- You immediately receive the maximum tax deduction that the IRS allows for that year, allowing you to time your charitable deductions.

- You have an option to name your DAF account advisors, as well as any successor donors or charitable beneficiaries which could help your children learn about philanthropy.

- Your contribution is placed into a DAF account, where it can be invested and grow tax-free.

---

18 "Donor-advised fund," Wikipedia, https://en.wikipedia.org/wiki/Donor-advised_fund.

- At any time afterward, you can recommend grants from your account to qualified charities. Most funds require the recipient charity to be a 501(c)(3) tax-exempt organization. There are some funds that may allow you to make gifts to international charities (with additional fees).

Case Study

Dr. Singh recently changed jobs and had a deferred compensation plan with $250,000 he had to withdraw. He and his wife were already doing some charitable giving. Rather than having $250,000 added to their regular income in that year and paying close to $100,000 in taxes, they chose to contribute $200,000 to a DAF and take a huge tax deduction. Whatever tax deduction they couldn't use that year carried forward for up to five years. They used those funds to make charitable gifts for many years to come. In addition to their contribution, Dr. Singh's new employer matched charitable contributions, so whenever they donated a certain amount to a charity, Dr. Singh's employer would also match that donation to a certain degree, allowing them to leverage their donations.

Another Thought about DAFs

Some DAFs also allow donations of appreciated stocks, bonds, or real estate. By donating appreciated assets, you may also gain the benefit of reducing or eliminating capital gains taxes and estate taxes.

Many people consider their DAFs to be their "make-a-friend" funds—that is, funds that they can use at future times to help out charitable causes or other friends who are working toward charitable goals. You also have an option of making anonymous gifts, if you wish. DAFs are a great way for most people to do charitable giving without the hassles of setting up their own charitable nonprofit organization.

DAFs are a great way for most people to do charitable giving without the hassles of setting up their own charitable nonprofit organization, which can be expensive to establish (due to legal fees) and also comes with a lot more ongoing administrative responsibilities. A DAF is a much easier way to accomplish some of your charitable goals.

Charitable Remainder Trusts

There are also some very interesting charitable trusts that allow you to make charitable gifts, take charitable tax deductions, and reduce or eliminate capital gains and estate taxes, all while allowing you to enjoy income benefits while living and passing on the remainder assets to the charities of your choice upon your death.

Case Study

Mr. and Mrs. Rao have created their wealth in real estate, and their net worth is estimated at $15 million. Mr. Rao also owns a parcel of property that he bought many years ago for $10,000, which is now worth about a million dollars. Mr. Rao would like to sell the land and possibly generate some income from the sale, but if he sells it he will have to pay capital gains taxes on $990,000. He and his wife are charitably inclined.

They agree to donate the land to a charitable remainder trust, which can later sell the land without any capital gains taxes. The Raos also receive a partial tax deduction for their donation. The trust invests the sale proceeds into an income-producing investment, which allows the Raos to take income for the rest of their lives. Upon their death, the trust's proceeds will go to their named charitable beneficiaries. The Raos can also name their DAF as their beneficiary, from which their children can make charitable gifts in the future. The result allows them to reduce their estate by $1 million, take some charitable deductions, generate income for life, and also support their charitable endeavors.

There is one slight problem. The Rao children are not happy that their inheritance is reduced by $1 million. Apparently, $14 million in possible inheritance wasn't enough for them. Haha! So the Raos also purchase a $1 million survivorship life insurance policy and keep it in a wealth-replacement insurance trust that will pay off $1 million to their children, free of income and estate taxes. Now, everyone is happy (except the IRS).

These are just some of the examples of what can be done with charitable giving. There are many other ways such as charitable lead trusts, as well as forming your own nonprofit organizations. If you are charitably inclined, you should consult a qualified professional who can assist you with your options.

CHAPTER 16

SIX LESSONS FOR MY KIDS AND YOU

Money is neither my god nor my devil. It is a form of energy that tends to make us more of who we already are, whether it's greedy or loving.

—DAN MILLMAN

Someone once asked the current Dalai Lama what surprises him the most about humanity, and his answer was pretty interesting. He said:

Man surprised me most about humanity. Because he sacrifices his health in order to make money. Then he sacrifices money to recuperate his health. And then he is so anxious about the future that he does not enjoy the present; the result being that he does not live in the present or the future; he lives as if he is never going to die, and then dies having never really lived.

We all know that money is important. Money gives us the freedom to experience and do many things while giving us a sense of security and power. But let's not forget that money isn't everything. There are billions of people in this world who have very little and still lead joyful lives. When you go to India and see the children in the streets playing, you can see the joy on their faces even though they may not have a shirt on their back.

Money is important! We need money to be able to do most of the things we want to do, whether it is traveling, retiring comfortably, or having nice things for ourselves and our family. One of the reasons I wanted to write this book was to pass on something for my kids as well as for you. If I had to sum up the most important lessons I want to pass on to my kids, they would be as follows:

1. **Money is an energy force:** Money is an energy force, and it deserves our respect. We have seen how economies thrive when money is present and flowing. We have also seen how they struggle when it is not. Money makes a lot of things possible. Realize that you need money in your life even if you are going to be on a spiritual path, but you don't need to let money own you.

2. **Remember the wheel of life:** The wheel of life has many sides, including Health and Well-Being, Personal Growth, Achievements, Work-Career, Friendship, Security, Energy, Self-Esteem, Fun and Recreation, Home-Family, Relationships, and of course, Finance. We need to pay attention to all areas of our lives, not just one or two.

If you would like to take an interesting test, take a look at the wheel of life diagram below. Notice that there are several spokes and a numerical scale, from zero to ten, in the middle.

Just for fun, rate all the different areas in your life from zero to ten. Be absolutely honest with yourself. No one else is going to see this unless you share it with them. This is just for you. Rate all of the areas from zero to ten, and then connect your dots.

THE WHEEL OF LIFE

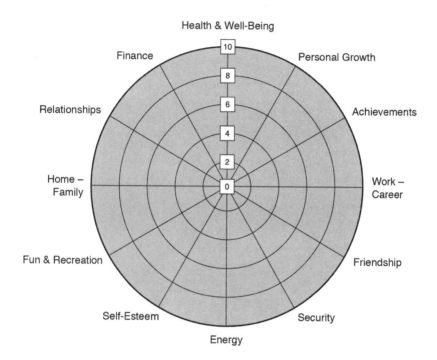

What does it look like? Is your wheel full in all areas of your life, or are you running a flat? Are there any areas where you could really use some work? Or are all areas pretty equal but just not as full as you would like them?

Now, create your bucket list. What are some of the things you want to do? Make a list of things that you want to have, do, and be, and get to work on accomplishing them.

I would recommend that you make the list and place it in your bathroom so that you can see it every day. It takes just as much effort to wish as it does to plan, so why not create the intention of doing a group of things that are the most important to you and check off the boxes?

3. Be unreasonable: When I look back on my life and the times that I have felt the most alive, those were the times when I was unreasonable with myself. Those were the times when I really pushed myself and stepped out of my comfort zone to do the things that were important to me in all areas of my life—physically, financially, mentally, and spiritually.

They say the comfort zone is a beautiful place, but nothing ever grows there. I think I would have to agree. I remember when we purchased our home: It was a bit out of our league, but we mustered up the courage to get it. It has been the best decision we could have made for our family, giving us a great neighborhood, great schools, and a beautiful house to raise our family.

The point is that when you really push yourself, you really feel alive! Have you ever pulled an all-nighter for something meaningful? Doesn't it stand out in your mind? As a matter of fact, it is 4:30 in the morning as I write this chapter because it feels good to do things out of your norm and be unreasonable with yourself. If nothing else, this will be memorable when I look back.

Think back to the people who have inspired you in your life. Chances are they were unreasonable in some way or another. People like Mahatma Gandhi, Martin Luther King Jr., or Steve Jobs had the audacity to be totally unreasonable with not only themselves but also the people around them. They expected more from themselves as well as from others. They didn't settle for mediocrity, and as a result they made a lasting impact in the lives of billions.

Go ahead and plan your ultimate retirement plan, and live the dream! Take a world cruise for a year if you wish. Live on the beach or in the mountains—whatever it is that will make you feel more alive.

Fear and doubts are terrible things. Fear kills more dreams than failure ever will. The mystics have told us that all fears are illusions. Danger may be real, but fear is optional. That is a great thing to keep in your mind. Danger may be real, but fear is optional. Remind yourself of this next time you want to shrink away from your dreams.

4. Stay in your financial reality: What I mean by this is "stay present." Don't worry so much about the future. Stay in the now! Many in our community came from very humble beginnings. You may be one of them. The conditioning we grew up with stays with us for life. Most of that conditioning comes from our parents, our environment, and our belief systems.

If you grew up believing that you have to be frugal about every-thing, you may find it difficult to spend money and really enjoy life. I know quite a few millionaires who lead very simple lives, and I don't think there is anything wrong with that, if that is what you really want. My father tends to be like that. He has his old clothes from thirty years ago and takes pride in still wearing them. Some people still drive their twenty-year-old car and are reluctant to buy a new one. If this gives you pleasure, please keep doing it!

All I am saying is, look at your current reality. If you have money, please enjoy your wealth! If you don't, then stay within your means. We have already talked about what can happen to your wealth after your passing. There is no guarantee that your money will be better used by your heirs or others. Many of you will be paying enormous amounts in taxes that may go to fund wars and other stupid things our taxes often pay for. Why not spend it on yourself and your family while you still have the chance?

5. Invest in yourself: Education never ends, whether it is for your career or for enrichment. There are always new, fun things to learn, even in retirement. As we have discussed earlier, our retirement may last for decades, and it would be nice to have many things you can learn and do to keep your mind and body active. So consider investing in yourself. The return on investment will be the enjoyment you derive from it.

If you are younger, invest in a coach or a physical trainer. Go back to school to learn something new that excites you. Write your book! Record your music album! I have now done all of these things, and I can tell you—it feels good!

6. Be generous: Our culture in India is based on negotiating for just about everything, and that instinct follows us everywhere we go. It is in our nature to seek bargains and try to maximize our benefits. I believe that, in certain areas of our lives, this is very important. But there are other areas where it is really not necessary—at least, not as much in this country. So why not be a little more generous, leave generous tips, and take care of the people who serve you on a regular basis?

What's the worst that can happen? You will make someone happy, and they might even treat you with more respect and consideration. If you own a business, be aware of other people's financial reality and, if possible, treat them with unexpected gifts and kindness.

Acknowledging the good that you already have in
your life is the foundation for all abundance.

—ECKHART TOLLE

Money has no memories! For my parting words, I would like to share an excerpt of an essay from an anonymous author that I came across many years ago, which beautifully conveys what I feel.

MONEY HAS NO MEMORIES. EXPERIENCE HAS.

You will never know what the total cost of your education was, but for a lifetime you will recall and relive the memories of schools and colleges. . . .

. . . You won't remember the cost of your honeymoon, but to the last breath you'll remember the experiences of the bliss of togetherness. . . .

Good times and bad times, times of prosperity and times of poverty, times when the future looked so secure and times when you didn't know from where the tomorrow will come life has been in one way or the other a roller-coaster ride for everyone. Beyond all that abundance and beyond all that deprivation, what remains is the memory of experiences. Sometimes the wallet was full. Sometimes even the pocket was empty. There was enough and you still had reasons to frown. There wasn't enough and you still had reasons to smile. . . .

No denying that anything that's material costs money, but the fact remains the cost of the experience will be forgotten, but the experience never will be. . . .

Time will pass, the economy will revive, currency will soon be in hand, and in all this, I don't want you to look back and realize you did nothing but stay in gloom. A recession can make you lose out on money. Let it not make you lose out on experiences. Choose to be happy and fulfilled with what you have and the law of attraction will be on your side to show you more things that you can be grateful for.

HOW CAN I HELP?

*If you don't build your dream, someone else
will hire you to help them build theirs.*

—DHIRUBHAI AMBANI

I hope you have enjoyed this book as much as I have enjoyed bringing it to you. I hope the information provided was helpful to you and brings value to your life. As I said in the introduction, this book represents the most important lessons I have learned during my twenty-five years in the financial-services industry.

The financial services are a challenging industry! Every day we have new crises. There is a constant flow of new products and changes in government and tax laws, and it is up to us as practitioners to keep up with the changes and to find the best solutions for our clients.

For those of you who are interested, my practice is divided into four main areas: insurance, investments, financial planning, and employee benefits. Although I can do many things and have licenses for all kinds of products, I try to stick to my strengths and the areas where I can provide the most value to our customers.

SURVEY: WHAT AREAS DO YOU FEEL YOU NEED THE MOST EDUCATION IN? CHECK ALL THAT APPLY.

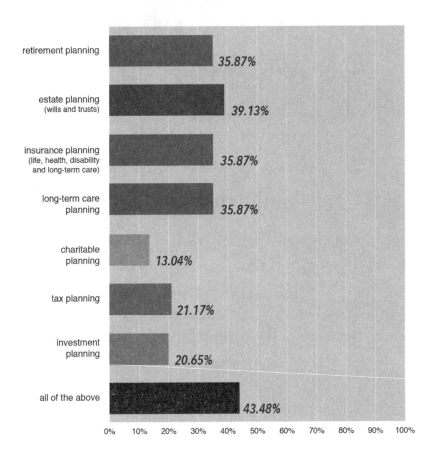

The name of my company is Shalin Financial Services, which is named after my oldest son Shalin, which means modest or humble. Our Shalin Financial mission statement is this:

"To provide our customers, our friends, with the best insurance and investment products in the marketplace, along with excellent customer service and an extraordinary level of knowledge and expertise for mutually rewarding, long-term relationships."

I believe that we are able to provide value to our customers by being an independent firm that can provide a wide spectrum of insurance and investment products from dozens of companies.

Here is a brief list of ways we can help you and your businesses. If we can be of assistance, please reach out to us.

Insurance planning: We represent dozens of top insurance companies for life, health, disability, long-term care, Medicare, and visitor health plans. By representing many insurance companies, we are able to provide our clients with a wide selection of products that are best suited for them. We do not charge any extra fees for our insurance products, as we are paid directly by the insurance companies we represent, and you as a consumer receive the same rates as if you went directly to the insurance company—but with the added value of our expertise to guide you and service your policy needs afterward.

You are welcome to learn more about our team by visiting our website at www.ShalinFinancial.com. There are a variety of resources available to you on our website, including free, instant term life quotes, health insurance quotes, and visitor health plan quotes. We recommend that you call us for specific product recommendations. Remember, our insurance services come to you at no extra cost, so why not take advantage?

Investment planning: As a securities broker, I am able to provide a wide variety of investment solutions for our clients based on their investment objectives. Additionally, as an investment advisor, I am considered a fiduciary and am held to higher standards of suitability. We offer products on both commission and fees, depending on the product and your needs.

Financial planning: The areas of financial planning where I can be of most value to you are insurance planning, retirement planning, estate planning, charitable planning, and tax-saving strategies for high-income earners. I offer a free, 15 minute consultation over the phone to discuss your needs. If I can help you, I will tell you my fees for additional services, and if I can't help you, I will try to refer you to other professionals who can serve you better.

Employee benefits: We help with group health insurance, retirement plans, and advanced planning for key employees and owners. By combining my financial-planning experience along with the benefits experience of our benefits partners at Regions Bank, we are able to help our clients find the most competitive benefits in the marketplace and stay in compliance (which is very important in the world of the Affordable Care Act). I have worked with Jennifer Stucky, Erin Dudley, and Dori Brilliant for more than fifteen years and couldn't ask for better partners to service our clients for their benefit needs and claims assistance throughout the year. With their assistance, we are able to serve large groups very effectively.

CONNECT WITH ME!

I send out a periodic e-mail newsletter to all of our clients with useful, timely information on various subjects, and I conduct free webinars on different products and financial-planning strategies. If you would like to be added to our e-mail newsletter, send me an e-mail at info@ RajeshJyotishi.com. You are also welcome to connect with me on Facebook, Twitter, and LinkedIn.

A FREE GIFT FOR YOU!

Someone once asked me, what would I do if I had just a year to live? My answer was, "Without hesitation, to finish my CD of songs I had written over the years." Several years ago, I had the privilege to work with some amazingly talented musicians and record my CD, *Carpe Diem*, which means "seize the day." The songs are in English in the pop and rock genre and have a motivational and inspirational feel to them.

My songs will tell you more things about me than I ever will. You can hear my songs and read my lyrics on my music website at www.RJ-Music.com. The CD is also available for purchase on iTunes, Amazon, and other online stores.

Namaste and thank you!

SURVEY RESULTS: WHAT ARE YOUR TWO BIGGEST WORRIES WHEN IT COMES TO RETIREMENT?

- Not having enough money and outliving my plans to live.

- Stock market uncertainty and wealth protection (estate planning).

- Deteriorating health and running out of savings.

- Will I have enough wealth for my retirement? What shall I do to minimize the tax effect of potential growth?

- That I'll be working until the day I die. I'll live a long time.

- What would happen if I fell terribly ill? Would my nest egg last me until I die?

- Not having saved enough hefty healthcare costs.

- Wiping out wealth for medical care or if I end up in a nursing home.

- Long-term care and health insurance.

- Inaccurately calculating the amount needed and unforeseen expenditures.

- Not enough time to save the proper amount of retirement money for a comfortable life. And anxiety over proper markets and companies to invest 401(k)/403(b) in when the stock markets can be so volatile.

- Being bored and having too little money for adventures.

- Income for day-to-day living and medical expenses.

- Money. After forty years of "money making" I'm now looking forward to hopefully forty years of "money spending" (retirement). How do I finance it? Health costs alone will eat up a fortune.

- Inflation-safe investments for senior years.

- Outliving our assets and health—as the saying goes, "Health is wealth."

- I don't worry about the future and that includes retirement.

- If I will have enough money for my lifestyle, as with modern medicine we live up to eighty to ninety-nine years. Basically the money made and saved in working life has to last for twenty years longer.

- Money market and economy.

- Living longer and not enough money to lead a comfortable lifestyle.

- Healthcare costs and understanding all the forms and government assistance for healthcare. When to retire and how much to take out each year—what type of lifestyle to lead.

- Will Social Security survive and would I be able to maintain my current lifestyle in retirement years?

- Health and standard of living.

- Not having enough money for fun activities like travel and eating out.

- Health and inflation.

MONEY TALK FOR TEENS

The following are just some of the answers from the survey I did for *The Money Talk for Teens*. I believe you will find this very interesting! If you would like to view the rest of the answers, go to www. RajeshJyotishi.com.

WHAT IS THE BEST ADVICE YOU HAVE EVER GOTTEN ON MONEY AND LIFE?

- The best advice that I have received is to save wisely and invest even more wisely. And money may not make your life happier but it sure makes it easier to be happier.

- Life, and how we live it, is far more important than money. We can be poor and happy if we live by a tried and true set of values. But if we earn much but are not so honorable we are as tinkling bells.

- For money: recognize your needs and wants and act on them accordingly. For life: know that everything happens for a reason and the way it is supposed to be.

- Should not spend more than one can afford. Always put some away as savings for a rainy day.

- Put a percentage of your income away for retirement. Pay off credit cards monthly. Do not keep a balance.

- While money is important, it is not everything. You need enough to live a somewhat comfortable life, but it should not be the end all be all. You need to be able to enjoy your life and treasure the things money cannot buy.

- Be generous. The more you give the more you get.

- Money is a river, never a lake. When we seek it, and hold it, it becomes stagnant. When we understand it is a river of blessing, it flows in and out a blessing for all concerned.

- The 30/70 rule: give 10 percent to charity, 10 percent to active investment, 10 percent to long-term investment, and 70 percent for living expenses.

- Don't work for money; make money work for you. Only way that's possible is to start saving and investing at an early age.

- Pay yourself first, i.e. save first, not after you have taken care of expenses. Start early—the magic of compounding will work wonders.

- Your self-identity does not come from how much money you make. Wear it like a loose garment.

- My grandfather used to say, "If you earn a dollar, spend twenty-five cents and save the rest." About life: look at people that have less than you and you will always be happy and content.

- Never ever borrow money for basic survival needs i.e. food/clothing/shelter. If you borrow money, that money must earn more than the basic prevailing interest.

- When making any significant purchase, always ask yourself the following question: Is this something I need or something I want? Asking this simple question has many times prevented me from wasting money. It helps me to be practical with my choices.

WHAT WOULD YOU TELL YOUR TEENAGER ON THE PRICE OF A COLLEGE EDUCATION?

- I would tell my teenager that it may seem like it costs a lot now, but it is the best investment you can make for yourself.

- It's an investment in their future.

- It can help. But it's all what you do with it or what you do without it

- Don't let the price discourage you. Once you educate yourself, that will be the highest price and wealth earned.

- Go to the best state school and take advantage of all scholarship opportunities. It does not make sense to graduate with $100k in student loans

- A college education is what you make of it. It can be a valuable preparation for the future or a waste of time and money. You determine how valuable it is.

- Invest in grad school, not undergrad.

- Just like everything else, there are good deals, bad deals, gold standards, and low standards. Do your research and find the best deal for your budget.

- Education is not only important but critical for living a fruitful life. But you do not have to get loans and spend money to go to Ivy League colleges to get educated. Public state universities are as good to open your mind and become productive members of society.

- That it's expensive, so choose wisely. You don't want a degree that is not marketable. After you get the degree that is marketable, then go ahead and do whatever else you like to do.

- It cannot be measured or quantified

- I will do my best to contribute toward your education, but please do not let it go to waste.

- This needs to be a multi-part question. What would you tell your teenager about choices regarding a college education? Public vs. private, in-state vs. out-of-state, size of college? What would you tell your teenager about preparing yourself to succeed in college? What would you tell your teenager preparing yourself to get a good financial aid package in college? What would you tell your teenager on the price of a college education?

- The price of a college education is growing every year, and with inflation counted, it is bound to grow higher. However, it's like planning a building construction. The stronger the foundation is the more floors you can build. If you work on strengthening your foundation then: 1) you can aim for a much higher education and 2) you can take advantage of scholarships to reduce the price of education.

- I started early with our sons. We started a college fund at birth for each of our sons. I told them constantly that I would help pay for college but not pay for their entire education. I felt it was important they had "skin in the game." As it turned out, they both worked since fourteen years old (I matched their savings until I couldn't) and they both paid $10k a year for their education. Both sons entered college and worked the entire time they were in college. One did co-op where he worked a semester and went to school for one semester. It made his college years longer, but when he finished he knew what he wanted to do and what he didn't want to do. Our other son majored in something that didn't offer co-op so he worked the entire time in college on the job he wanted after college.

WHAT ADVICE WOULD YOU GIVE YOUR TEENAGER WHO WANTS TO ENTER THE ARTS, ACTING, MUSIC, OR SPORTS?

- Doing what you like to do will bring happiness and success and life will be more meaningful and easier.

- I would fully support and encourage them but advise them to have a fallback option if things don't work out.

- I made my son create a spreadsheet of his expenses that we cover and then added hypothetical expenses for the future (rent, insurance, car payment, etc.) Then we told him that he needed to choose a career that would allow him to earn enough money to live the lifestyle he desires.

- Give it 100 percent passionate effort, but be honest with yourself about your potential.

- Absolutely! I'm delighted as long as they are committed to it and willing to put in the effort to become outstanding. The world needs people of every skill, and folks in all of these fields can do well if they can differentiate themselves. The key is that education and work is about how to live and life. I want my kids to know that learning to design a life that they want to live is important.

- Follow your dreams and passion. Do what you enjoy but figure out what will pay your bills

- To follow their dreams but to also know enough to manage the reality of the dream. You may have to struggle, so it is good to have a backup plan in case things don't work out, especially with sports where injuries can make or break a career.

- Absolutely do it! But know that there is a time window and a plan B is needed. Do what you are good at not solely for the money. But also be reasonable and realistic. Set a time goal of how much time you are willing to put into this dream.

- Follow your heart but take your head with you. Make sure your basic needs are covered before you follow your passion.

- What do you see yourself doing in five years? In ten years? If they respond in the arts or sports arena they wish to pursue, help them to see what funding and scholarships are available to support their endeavor in addition to the college fund I would have set up for them. Let them know there is a limit and a deadline to seeking a successful life and get them to define what is a success and come to that agreement. Get them to read, think about it, and then sign that agreement with you. Review that agreement each year until they are seniors in high school.

- Ahhh, that is a controversial one. Getting into arts, acting, music, or sports is acceptable as long as you do not sacrifice time to learn a skill to earn your living. I do not appreciate artists, actors, musicians, or sportsmen who become a "burden" on society or complain about wealthy, successful engineers, doctors, or businessmen. These artists, actors etc. fail to see the sacrifices engineers/doctors/businessmen have made.

- Follow your dream; just don't get into debt for it.

- Study business as well, and be willing to alter your dream to work in your desired field but perhaps not be a "star." I have a masters in painting. I rarely paint anymore. But I use that knowledge every day in my job as an art director and photo stylist. And I'm happier doing this than painting every day, but I would never have gotten here without pursuing that creative path.

- It is your life and you have to follow your interests and talents. Life is too short to follow a career that someone else has chosen for you. At the same time, you must realize that most people who are in such fields do not make close to the income that others in traditional fields such as engineering, finance, medical etc. might make. You have to be willing to live within your income. You might have to be more creative, but that does not mean that you will enjoy life less.

- Well, it is a great idea if you are willing to deal with failure of not making it to the top (99.999 percent). At that point, you may have to start all over in another career that pays better or deal with living off of low paychecks.

- Do it, just realize that very few people are successful in those fields and it is often short lived. Have a plan B ready in case it doesn't work out or even if you decide you don't like that anymore!

WHAT ADVICE WOULD YOU GIVE YOUR TEENAGER ON MARRIAGE AND MONEY?

- I would advise my teenager that a marriage shouldn't be focused around money or even the choice in spouse. However, it is a critical part of it in that both partners have to be on a similar page when it comes to spending and saving.

- Money should be secondary to love/marriage, maybe even separate. Unless they have similar thoughts on money, it's something that will take years to compromise and manage money well in a marriage.

- Stand on your own two feet first, have a career and savings, and make sure you split the cost of the wedding with your soulmate. Marriage is an institution, so follow the rules and regulations that go along with it.

- Talk about the important things in life before getting married to see if you are really compatible. For example: to have kids or not, how many, when to have them, how to raise them, where to live, what type of jobs and ambitions to have, when to retire, etc. Write them down. Sit down with your potential spouse but also with someone else (like a counselor).

- Create a budget for the event. Plan for the first five years of married life. Build a pyramid of assets like real-estate, life insurance, investments, travel budget, hobby budget, etc.

- Don't rush into marriage and do it when you are ready. I would discourage spending tons of money on a wedding when it could be used for saving and future.

- Do what you love, love what you do, is a choice in marriage, too, but now it takes two. Don't do it for the money. Do it to finish it.

- Don't ever marry for money. Don't marry just to be married. Life is a journey—experience and enjoy each stage.

- Remember marriage is followed by financial responsibility

- To girls, always, always be financially independent. It will make you a stronger spouse. Men can get sick, lose their jobs, die, leave you, etc. Don't risk your and your kids' financial security.

- Communication is key to a good relationship. Talk openly to your partner about money and how you both plan to save and spend it.

- Don't go in debt over a wedding, and spend the money on a home instead, and make certain you and the person you marry see eye-to-eye on finances.

- On marriage, remember that you are a team. It's all about compromising and meeting halfway. When money is involved both have to be on the same page and make smart financial decisions. Those smart decisions will help you when you both decide to have a family.

- No chokri without naukri—get on your own feet, put aside a decent amount of savings, and make sure you can support three before committing to marriage. Also try to donate part of the amount you would have spent on your wedding and invest the rest in a college savings plan for your kids.

- Marriage is a journey of two soulmates until the end of life. It is carving a path for themselves as well as their offspring for a better life. No two people are alike but still marriage holds them together by giving the opportunity to complement each other with their strengths and weaknesses. And marriage is a responsibility of giving proper education to the future generation so money is very important for the life planning.

- On marriage, become friends first. Don't compromise on the things that are important to you before marriage, but do compromise once you are married. Marriage is never a 50/50 proposition. Sometimes you will give 80 percent and receive 20 percent and sometimes you receive 90 percent and give only 10 percent. Just be sure it balances out over the long haul and even the short haul. On money, it's important, but never let it drive your career decisions. Choose jobs based on the content of the assignment— make sure you will enjoy it. Work for companies who share your values. Shakespeare said, "Let the firstlings of my heart be the firstlings of my hand."

WHAT ADVICE WOULD YOU GIVE YOUR TEENAGER
ON SPENDING AND FRUGALITY?

- I would advise my teenager to spend as needed and minimize wants versus needs. Regarding frugality, I would teach him/her how to find the best deals and ways to save money.

- Work hard and play hard. If they are willing to work for what they want and spend how they want, I'd be okay with that. I would hope there is a level of appreciation so they wouldn't live outside of their means. The long-term picture isn't always easy for teenagers to see/understand without understanding the struggles.

- Spend below your means. If you make money, then buy good things that will last and you will enjoy.

- Life is meant to be enjoyed. You can't take up snow skiing when you are seventy-five or hit your favorite party cities. Similarly you have to save for your future. Prioritize where you spend your money.

- Spend less than you make. Learn to invest and use money as a tool. Do not let money drive your life, let your life drive the money. Have at least a one-year emergency fund and save a minimum of 25–50 percent of what you make.

- Spend when it is necessary, but do not throw away when you find no values. Avoid too much impulse spending. Maximize value by marketing promotions, coupons, etc.

- Enjoy life and put aside a certain percentage of your income. Buy a few nice things that will last you a long time versus lots of inexpensive things.

- Set your goals and reward yourself. Spent wisely and take some time to think about it before you make big purchases. Do your research on pricing.

- If you want to have financial security, live beneath your means. Create a budget and track your spending. Spend money on experiences and relationships that will last a lifetime rather than on "things."

- Spend wisely but don't be frugal. You don't want to have a million dollars at one point and regret that you didn't enjoy it when you could have.

- You don't have to have the latest and greatest. However, I believe it is important to treat yourself occasionally to little things to reward yourself for handwork. Don't try to keep up with those around you. There will always be someone with bigger and better things than you. Count your blessings and be grateful you aren't homeless!

- Spend but spend wisely. And be prepared to earn according to your necessity to spend

- There's always going to be something that makes you want to have. Obviously you cannot own them all. Make sure you know the difference between "want it" and "need it."

- Control spending. In this materialistic society, control your temptation to buy only items you require unless those items are strictly required. Be frugal, if you can save a penny, do not be embarrassed to start saving that penny.

- Income is not wealth. What you keep is more important than what you earn. Avoid conspicuous consumption and keeping up with the Joneses.

- Always make decisions based on value, not the absolute cost.

- If one has to feed oneself on a mountain, soon the mountain will be melted to a flat land. There is a fine distinction between spending versus spending wisely. Check before you spend: 1) If you don't buy this item today, would there be any regrets? 2) Is it an investment or expense? In the sense, is this going to contribute to your personal growth? 3) Treat money with respect so that you place it in good hands or spend it for a good cause.

- Be frugal to a point, but do not miss out on an opportunity if it is following your dreams.

- Frugality is a skill that must be learnt, practiced, and polished constantly. Spending will become sensible naturally.

WHAT WOULD YOU TELL YOUR TEENAGER ON DEBT?

- Know the difference between good debts and bad debts.

- Live debt free. You will have less worries in the long run. Some debt is unavoidable like college loans, mortgage. No credit card debt.

- Debt is best kept to a minimum in your life

- Debt is horrible. Once you get into debt, it's very hard to come out. Don't live beyond your means. Debt is meant for emergencies, not a lifestyle choice.

- Avoid debt except for a business, house, or other appreciating asset.

- Debt can ruin lives, marriages, and overall happiness. Prioritize your spending, and never buy something you cannot afford.

- Try to keep away from useless debt. Be judicious; some debts are necessary for financial growth.

- Avoid it like the plague, but know and understand, debt can be a tool but only for those disciplined enough to use it as such.

- Debt is a two-sided sword. You can highly leverage it and make a lot of money or struggle to balance your budget.

- Debt is not necessary.

- Debt will ruin your life. It can have a chokehold on your adult life. The trick is to save properly and never get into any serious debt. House and car? Okay. Don't get sucked into credit card hell.

- Do not use your car or home as an ATM.

- Pay off your debt as soon as possible.

- Never get into a debt you cannot pay off.

- Debt is not bad, but follow a couple of principles before you sign on the dotted line. 1) Clearly identify the reason why you want to take debt. 2) Do you have a viable plan to pay off the debt? 3) Do you clearly understand the risks of delinquency? Summary: Taking a loan for a five-star world cruise for your honeymoon at $50k on your credit card at a 30 percent interest is bad if your salary is $24k/year and you have no assets, living in a one-bedroom rental apartment.

- Everyone at some point has it. It's up to you to make sure it does not get out of hand. There will always be expenses that come up, but again just know how to handle it.

- Debt is not necessarily bad and depends on purpose. E.g. debt for home may be okay since you are paying an affordable amount for enjoying a higher quality of life and building equity versus rent throwaway. And debt used for business with a higher ROI (compared to cost of debt) is justified.

- Never ever borrow money for basic needs: food/clothing/ shelter. If you borrow money, that money must earn more than the basic prevailing interest.

- Never make minimum payment of charge card bills— never. Pay it off in full every month.

- Take it one day and one dollar at a time. Debt can accrue quickly and can take a tremendous amount of time to get back to zero. Take your credit score seriously, from the moment that first credit card application is submitted. Your credit will open and close doors, specifically in the United States.

- Debt is like a medicine you take to cure yourself of an ailment. Obviously, you don't want to be on medicines for a long time. Either you take the right dosage of medicine for the right duration or create a healthy lifestyle that you don't have to depend on medicines. Similarly, you want to create a situation where you don't need debt. However, if you have to, try to repay it as soon as possible because the longer the debt the greater the side effects of it.

WHAT ADVICE WOULD YOU GIVE YOUR TEENAGER ON SAVING AND INVESTING?

- Saving is good; save a portion in deposits, a portion in investments. Do all the available research on investing before jumping into one.

- Start saving early and often. If you are earning, then set up an automatic withdrawal into a mutual fund or into a retirement plan.

- Learn to invest and manage your money as much as possible. Start as early as you can.

- Saving is not enough. One has to invest to get enough return to last a lifetime. Learn early, try early, and fail fast. Be flexible and disciplined about both saving and investing. Read a lot and educate yourself about investing from the very best in the industry.

- Start saving at an early age for your retirement.

- Save 10 percent first before paying anything else. Invest the money in something that grows faster than inflation, such as equity funds or real estate investment properties. Diversify risk.

- Saving and investing while at the end may be all meant for taking care of the future, it is important that they balance the amounts. Do not invest in any one instrument.

- Keep six to nine months of income in the bank just in case you lose your job or have any unforeseen circumstances. The stock markets are way too volatile to trust.

- Put away the max in 401(k) and IRA, especially from earliest age possible.

- Get a really good, trustworthy advisor.

- Save 25 percent of your paycheck

- Do the numbers. Ten years of saving and investing in your twenties beats twenty years of the same in your forties every time.

- You need to save money for several events: "rainy days" and retirement. You need at least six months of liquid assets to handle potential job loss/health issues/accidents/etc. Retirement investment should be built into every dollar of compensation. Investing should be built like a pyramid, investing in protected assets at the bottom and increasing risk/return with lesser amounts up the pyramid.

- Put aside savings on long-term assets; put aside a third of your savings on safe investments, a third on medium-risk investments, and balance on slightly riskier investments till the age of fifty. After that, invest 50 percent each on the first two categories and shy away from risk-oriented investments.

- Have a balanced, long-term approach to saving and investing. Heed the advice of Warren Buffet, the world's greatest investor. He said, "I don't invest in something that I do not understand."

- Start saving in your teen years. Automate your savings so that you will not be tempted to spend the money, and it will feel painless. Take full advantage of every tax-sheltered opportunity like 401(k)s, HSAs, FSAs, etc.

- I shared our savings and investing with our kids at an early age. It doesn't start as teenagers. It starts with always speaking openly and honestly about money. They need to understand that an expense with a car includes gas, insurance, tires, and maintenance. They also need to know they have to work for whatever they want.

- Good investment is the closest thing to a tree on which money grows. But you need to plant the seeds at a very young age and nourish it over time so it can become a tree that keeps on giving.

WHAT WOULD YOU TELL YOUR TEENAGER ON WELFARE AND ENTITLEMENT PROGRAMS?

- I would tell my teenager that there are programs such as welfare and entitlement programs that help those in need but that everyone should try do their part to minimize his/her impact by becoming more fiscally responsible.

- They exist to help those who need it, and it should be temporary.

- Only use it in extreme needs. We are proud people.

- All of us can be in an unfortunate situation, needing temporary help without any advance notice. So do not look down on people who might be on welfare, etc. However, I want to impress that you do everything in your power to never have to be on welfare, etc. Stand on your own two feet and help someone else beyond yourself.

- Government does not owe you anything. Stand on your own feet! Learn to fish at an early age and you will have plenty of fish to last you your lifetime!

- Try to get out of welfare as soon as possible and do not expect someone to hand over stuff to you. Earn what you desire and deserve.

- Welfare and entitlement programs are there for dire situations. For long term, they just keep you living in poverty and do not foster self-esteem.

- It makes one lazy and dependent.

- That people on welfare are not less intelligent or less capable or a burden. It is in the government's responsibility to help those on the margins and it's not a hand out but a step up.

- I'm not sure how I feel about the use of entitlement programs. Some people have hard times and different challenges. They are there to help people get on their feet and take care of their children. It is a safety net when things are tough. Not everyone has access to it and it is harder to get than most people realize.

- Some people deserve it and some abuse it. Look at it from both sides

- Such programs will only make you weaker in pursuing your goals for a financially secured life. Don't even consider such programs or else you may become lazy.

- Use it when in crisis.

- Welfare is for people who are trying to recover from unfortunate circumstances. Please work hard enough to avoid welfare. However, in case you need to; please attempt to reach out to all other sources of assistance before claiming welfare.

- They are important to any society. We have had family members that have had to rely on food stamps or reduced lunch programs to survive hard times. It's not what you want to do, but its good if you need it.

- Plan so you never have to be on welfare. And if you do wind up on unemployment, I do not agree with the term "entitlement." In this case, or if it is referring to Social Security, as employees, that's what we have paid into these programs for.

- I will advise my teenager to grow a sense of pride and self-dependency. Welfare and entitlement programs are available so that the citizens can survive until they are on their feet again. The enjoyment and satisfaction a child will get after making purchases with their own money cannot be compared with things showered on them by others.

- Whatever the government can give you, the government can take away from you.

- Do not depend on these. They are here today. Tomorrow they might be gone.

- Everyone is responsible for his or her own actions.

- Hard times could come upon anybody. Society has these programs to take care of people, but don't abuse it and count on it. Take pride in yourself and do the right things.

- They are there for a reason. If you face hardship, say unexpected sickness, loss of job, etc., don't feel shy to use the safety net.

- Don't count on them. If you get any help from government in your old age, treat it as icing on the cake. But let that not be a part of your retirement plan.

WHAT WOULD YOU TELL YOUR TEENAGER ON EXPECTING AN INHERITANCE FROM YOU?

- I would tell my teenager that the money that I have saved may eventually be passed down as an inheritance, but do not expect it. He/she needs to work as hard as I did and not expect free money from me.

- Not to expect one. They should work for what they want and need in life, and if they do get something, it will be discussed near my end of life.

- Again, write your own future. We will be leaving everything to you and your siblings, but don't depend on that.

- There will be an inheritance, but live your life as if you weren't getting one.

- It is something that they should expect as a pleasant surprise but not totally rely on them.

- Focus on accumulating wealth on your own. Don't be dependent on inherited monies.

- Don't hold your breath.

- Not to expect any. If as parents we helped you get an education, you should be able to stand on your own and not need our inheritance. However, if in the unfortunate situation, you wasted your life away in spite of our effort, also you do not need our inheritance, as it would be wasted.

- Go make your own legacy. Don't wait on my inheritance. It might not even be there when I am done retiring!

- Ha! April Fools!

- I would tell them to conduct their lives as if I will die a billionaire and leave everything to charity.

- Your education is your inheritance so make your own life.

- If you receive an inheritance, consider it as a windfall bonus, as if I am likely to donate my assets/savings toward charity.

- Each generation has to earn for his or her own survival, just like animals in the wild.

- Plan your life as though there is nothing coming to you. Anything can happen between now and then, and it is best to learn early on that you must become self-reliant. Nothing is promised in life except change and death.

- Sorry kiddo. You're on your own. My job was to provide you with the love, support, and education that you need to become a productive member of society, capable of taking care of yourself. I think I did a fabulous job. Now, if you don't mind, I'm heading to Hawaii and will be spending your inheritance. I want to croak with less than a thousand bucks in my bank account. I'm joking a little, but not too much!

- I tell my sons they will not inherit anything from us, but I give them things now. They have seen my great grandmother live to be 101 and my grandmother is still alive at 100. All their money has gone to end-of-life care. They see that the money my grandparents had was used to give them great quality of life—it wasn't for their heirs.

WHAT WOULD YOU TELL YOUR TEENAGER ABOUT GIVING AND GENEROSITY?

- I would tell my teenager that giving and generosity is part of the full circle of being a good citizen and human being. The more you give, the more you will receive back.

- Always be kind and helpful whenever and wherever you can.

- Giving is the ultimate way of happiness.

- To give and hope they have the ability to give. Do so frequently to the right people and organizations. There are always less fortunate people in this world, and helping someone could change their lives (both people).

- We need to work hard and earn and return back to the community and help the needy. This is very, very, very important.

- Be generous. Charity is important, but there are more ways to give to charity than just money. Time, I think, is more important and valuable and if you give your time to causes you believe in, it may be more rewarding.

- Do it with your hands. Do not give to other people to donate on your behalf.

- Charity starts at home. Take care of family first.

- Give, give, give and don't expect anything in return. Do it from the goodness of your heart.

- Giving blesses the receiver and the giver.

- Real deep satisfaction in life only comes when we go beyond ourselves. Life is all about giving and never shy away from it, be it your time, money, talent, etc.

- Give back to the society that has given you so much.

- Giving is it's own reward. It's not just about money. Forgiveness, energy, time—the possibilities (for giving) are endless.

- Tithe and support causes you believe in. Volunteer your time and your talents. To whom much is given much is expected.

- Be generous. The more you give the more you get. Money is not the root of happiness. Helping others and showing love through generosity is the greatest payoff as it relates to money.

- Giving brings pleasure. What goes around comes around.

- You benefit from someone's pull who is ahead of you in life. You benefit by experiencing the world by standing on other people's shoulders. You should offer the same to some other people. Don't break that chain. On the contrary, keep it going—strong and shiny.

- Be generous to people who need your generosity. Do not give to show off your wealth or due to peer pressure. Give only to good causes. If you are needy yourself, do not feel the pressure to give monetarily; you can always give through actions and help.

- Pay it forward.

- Always give as much as you can comfortably afford to charity. It will come back to you in the end. There are many people in the world who end up in situations that they had no control over. We as individuals and members of society must take care of them. Not the government but as private citizens.

- Karma is real. Give when you can financially, even if it is a dollar at the checkout line or to a child selling candy for a fundraiser. Remember that the few dollars you offer goes a long way to the recipient. Giving time and compassion can be more valuable. Volunteer whenever you can. You can enrich your life with fancy things, people, fame, fortune, materials of all sorts, but how do you enrich your soul? By giving a piece of yourself to others in the form of kindness.

- Giving is not a choice. It is our duty.

WHAT DO YOU EXPECT FROM YOUR CHILDREN IN YOUR OLD AGE?

- I expect nothing, but I hope they will take care of me as I did for them growing up. I don't think I will need them to financially take care of me, but I would like to have a strong relationship with them.

- Nothing but to be treated with kindness and love as we did for them in their childhood.

- Compassion, tolerance, understanding! I know they will be there with me every step of my life.

- Regular get-togethers.

- Love.

- To show up to my house with their families at least once per year and to call once a week.

- That they call me and visit when they can and let me spend time with my grandkids.

- Listen to us and acknowledge our feelings, love and caring for us.

- We have plans for our old age. Do not worry; we do not expect anything from you.

- Nothing financially, but I expect a close relationship with my children. I would like to be financially independent, and I want my kids to be financially independent. As a parent, I want to have a strong relationship with my children and grandchildren so that they will want to visit and spend time with me in my old age.

- Access to meet them frequently and opportunity to pamper our grandchildren. Also chances to provide relief to our children so they can leave kids behind with us and go on vacations.

- Love, respect, and aid if requested. Think Golden Rule.

- Love, compassion, companionship, assistance, and if needed to take care of my affairs if I am unable.

- Give me the emotional support I may need. I will do my best to be financially independent. Don't put me in an old age home; I didn't put you twenty-four hours in a childcare center!

- I expect them to communicate frequently and plan reasonable visits. I strive to stay independent as much as I can, but if I cannot live alone, I would expect them to help me make the proper decision about living arrangements, caretaking etc. We take care of our kids, and they must bear some responsibility for helping us out when we no longer can manage alone.

- Love. Nothing more, not care, nor money nor "repayment" of anything. As parents, we do out of love, not expecting any repayment. Let me cherish the love of my grandkids.

- I have purchased long-term health care and have saved money from the age of fifteen. I don't expect my children to take care of me. I have planned and will continue to plan so my kids don't have to financially support me.

IN YOUR OWN WORDS, LIST THREE MAIN THINGS YOU WOULD LIKE FOR ME TO CONVEY IN THIS BOOK ON MONEY AND THE WHEEL OF LIFE ON YOUR BEHALF.

- Balancing family, finances, and personal life is very important. Even though we all know about it, different phases of life bring different challenges. We just need to do our best every day and not have any regrets for what we did or what we did not do.

- They will get a lot of advice in life. Always do your research and stay close to honest, smart people. No matter what you do, be happy. Doesn't matter what career, friends, or things you have, without true happiness it's a pointless journey. Take risks and frequently as you can or can afford. Mistakes will happen, but the ride and unknown outcomes that may come is the reason I live. We have one life, and if you cruise through it, it's no fun!

- Our thoughts are the sole-creating source of our prosperity. Be mindful of the quality of the thoughts we are thinking. Adopt and maintain a God mind-set that we come into this world financed by God, with all that we desire or required already on our pathway. Never waiver in our faith. The supply is released through faith.

- We are very fortunate to live in the USA. We have so much that we should not complain. Live life simply and you will have little worries. Live below your means and find out what your passions are and pursue them.

- Life moves in a circle, and it is best not to spend your entire life chasing money otherwise you will go around in circles without experiencing the joys of life. Take care of your money and it will surely take care of you and your family in times of need. Pay attention to saving by investing starting when you are young, as there is no better ROI than the power of compound interest.

- There should be a balance between being frugal and an overspender. Biggest lesson I learned was from the death of my mother. She traveled her whole life and went to all the places she could. If she had waited or saved her whole life it would have been too late. As my father says, as time goes on and the older you get you value different things. Travel, partying, and even material things matter very little. Your memories are forever; make sure you have a life that is full of them.

- Money should never be a criteria to live life. I heard from many that you spend less than 10 percent of what you earn on yourself. So while young, spend time and money on learning. As an adult, apply yourself to be best in everything. It will automatically bring fame, respect, and prosperity. Never forget to support people around you in any way you can, and make it purposeful toward later parts of life.

- Set goals in every area of life, and work hard to achieve those goals. Create a budget and track your spending. If you want to have financial security, live beneath your means, and start investing early.

- Money is an instrument to cater to your needs and needs to be managed well. However good or bad a situation is, it will change. We cannot control the wind, but we can control the sails.

- Live a life that has meaning. Stand on your feet. Explore and live life to the fullest.

- Money is important. Life is more important. Living is most important.

- While money is essential, there is a lot more to life than money. Education is the best investment you will ever make but doesn't necessarily translate to success. Some of the most successful people had no formal education. Some of the happiest people in the world are also the poorest and most illiterate.

- Whether you like it or not, money is an extremely important part of life, and it is necessary to earn at certain levels to maintain a lifestyle that allows you to maintain happiness. Having money gives you options and allows you to accomplish things that you may not be able to without it. As important as money is, it is not the "end all." People, and how you treat others, are what is most important. Never put too much emphasis on money and material things. They are ultimately irrelevant. Your family, your friends, and your community are what really matter most.